✦ AEROFILMS GUIDE

# FOOTBALL
## GROUNDS

**AEROFILMS GUIDE**

**FOURTH REVISED EDITION**

# FOOTBALL
## GROUNDS

**DIAL HOUSE**

# CONTENTS

**Page 1: The Cellnet Riverside Stadium, home of Middlesbrough, was the only wholly new stadium to open for the 1995/96 season. Replacing the familiar Ayresome Park, home to the club since 1903, the new stadium was a suitable venue for the multi-national talents brought to Tees-side by Bryan Robson.**

**Page 3: With an all-seating capacity of more than 55,000 Old Trafford is a fitting home for Alex Ferguson's double winning Manchester United team.**

First published in 1993
Reprinted 1993 (Twice)
Second edition 1994
Third edition 1995
Fourth edition 1996

ISBN 0 7110 2489 X

Published by Dial House

an imprint of Ian Allan Ltd, Terminal House, Station Approach, Shepperton, Surrey KT15 1HY

Printed by Ian Allan Printing Ltd, Coombelands House, Addlestone, Weybridge, Surrey KT15 1HY

Aerial photography ©

Aerofilms

Hunting Aerofilms Limited have been specialists in aerial photography since 1919. Their library of aerial photographs, both new and old, is in excess of 1.5 million images. Aerofilms undertake to commission oblique and vertical survey aerial photography which is processed and printed in their specialised photographic laboratory. Digital photomaps are prepared using precision scanners. The Company has been a subsidiary of Hunting plc since 1936.

Free photostatic proofs are available on request for any site held within the collection and price lists will be forwarded detailing the sizes of photographic enlargement available without obigation to purchase.

Text © Ian Allan Ltd 1993, 1994, 1995, 1996
Football action photography © Empics
Photographs of Wembley reproduced by kind permission of Wembley plc

# Editor's Note

Welcome to the fourth edition of the *Aerofilms Guide: Football Grounds*. As before the book has been updated to take account of the changes that have affected the grounds in the FA Carling Premiership and the Nationwide Leagues. Each year, we think that the number of improvements will diminish, but such is the rate of change that more than a third of the grounds illustrated have undergone some alteration. In some cases this is perhaps no more than cosmetic; in others the grounds have been radically altered through the construction of new stands. Amongst those grounds that have changed dramatically are those at Preston North End, Carlisle United and Manchester United, whilst Bristol Rovers has abandoned Bath in favour of sharing a ground with Bath Rugby Club in the north of the city.

In compiling this book, the publishers endeavour to make the book as up to date as possible. However, modern construction methods mean that stands can appear almost overnight and it is therefore inevitable that there will be further changes to certain grounds by the start of the season. To illustrate this point, it was reported towards the end of the season that one club was replacing a terrace with a new stand and that this stand was expected to be completed close to the start of the new season. An aircraft was specially sent to photograph the new construction; the resulting photographs showed the old terrace still standing and the new season less than two months away! Whether the new stand will appear by August only time will tell.

Looking to the future, it would appear that the revolution in football grounds shows no signs of abating. More clubs are planning on abandoning their traditional grounds and building new all-seater stadia; the 1997/98 season is likely to see teams as far apart as Sunderland, Derby and Oxford all based at new grounds. Other clubs will be continuing to upgrade their existing stadia; Middlesbrough are already proposing to construct corner stands at the new Cellnet Riverside Stadium, for example, and Preston intend to rebuild progressively at Deepdale.

Unfortunately, it has been decided to drop the Scottish section from this edition of the guide; the costs involved in including the extra information would have made the book's cover price prohibitive. We hope that the omission will not mar your enjoyment of the book or reduce its usefulness.

As before, we would like to thank the majority of clubs who have been very helpful in confirming data and providing information on future developments. We hope that the information published is correct, but if there are any errors please contact the editor, c/o Ian Allan Publishing, Coombelands House, Addlestone, Weybridge KT15 1HY.

We hope that you will have an enjoyable season of watching football and that the new season will bring your team success (except perhaps in the event of them playing the editor's own favourites!).

# WEMBLEY

## Wembley Stadium, Wembley HA9 0DW

**Tel No:** 0181-902 8833
**Advance Tickets Tel No:** 0181-900 1234
**Brief History:** Inaugurated for F.A. Cup Final of 1923, venue for many major national and international matches including World Cup Final of 1966. Also used for major occasions in other sports and as venues for rock concerts and other entertainments.
**(Total) Current Capacity:** 79,000 (all seated)
**Nearest Railway Station:** Wembley Complex (BR), Wembley Central (BR & Tube), Wembley Park (tube)

**Parking (Car):** Limited parking at ground and nearby
**Parking (Coach/Bus):** As advised by police
**Police Force:** Metropolitan
**Anticipated Development(s):** Wembley is one of two sites being examined in connection with a proposed new national stadium. If Wembley gets the nod over the rival site in Manchester, the existing stadium will be redeveloped.

# ARSENAL

## Arsenal Stadium, Avenell Road, Highbury, London, N5 1BU

**Tel No:** 0171 704 4000
**Advance Tickets Tel No:** 0171 704 4040
**League:** F.A. Premier
**Brief History:** Founded 1886 as Royal Arsenal, changed to Woolwich Arsenal in 1891, and Arsenal in 1914. Former grounds: Plumstead Common, Sportsman Ground, Manor Ground (twice), moved to Arsenal Stadium (Highbury) in 1913. Record attendance 73,295
**(Total) Current Capacity:** 38,000 (all seated)
**Visiting Supporters' Allocation:** 2,600 (all seated)

**Club Colours:** Red shirts with white sleeves, white shorts
**Nearest Railway Station:** Drayton Park & Finsbury Park. Arsenal (tube)
**Parking (Car):** Street Parking
**Parking (Coach/Bus):** Drayton Park
**Police Force and Tel No:** Metropolitan (0171 263 9090)
**Disabled Visitors' Facilities**
  **Wheelchairs:** Lower tier East Stand
  **Blind:** Commentary available
**Anticipated Development(s):** none planned.

### KEY

**C** Club Offices
**E** Entrance(s) for visiting supporters

⬆ North direction (approx)

❶ Avenell Road
❷ Highbury Hill
❸ Gillespie Road
❹ To Drayton Park BR Station (¼ mile)
❺ Arsenal Tube Station
❻ Clock End

*Left:*
One of a number of high-profile overseas players to make their mark in English football during the 1995/96 season, the Dutch international Dennis Bergkamp made his presence felt for an Arsenal team then managed by Bruce Rioch. Despite the arrival of Bergkamp and former England captain David Platt, Arsenal never really threatened in any competition.

# ASTON VILLA

## Villa Park, Trinity Road, Birmingham, B6 6HE

**Tel No:** 0121 327 2299
**Advance Tickets Tel No:** 0121 327 5353
**League:** F.A. Premier
**Brief History:** Founded in 1874. Founder Members Football League (1888). Former Grounds: Aston Park and Lower Aston Grounds & Perry Barr, moved to Villa Park (a development of the Lower Aston Grounds) in 1897. Record attendance 76,588
**(Total) Current capacity:** 39,300 (all seated)
**Visiting Supporters' Allocation:** Approx. 2,567 (all seated) in the Witton End 'R' block
**Club Colours:** Claret with blue stripe shirts, white shorts.

**Nearest Railway Station:** Witton
**Parking (Car):** Asda car park, Aston Hall Road
**Parking (Coach/Bus):** Asda car park, Aston Hall Road (special coach park for visiting supporters situated in Witton Lane).
**Police Force and Tel No:** West Midlands (021) 322 6010
**Disabled Visitors' Facilities**
  **Wheelchairs:** Trinity Road Stand section
  **Blind:** Commentary by arrangement
**Anticipated Development(s):** With the completion of seating at the Holte End, no further work is planned.

### KEY

**C** Club Offices
**S** Club Shop
**E** Entrance(s) for visiting supporters
**R** Refreshment bars for visiting supporters
**T** Toilets for visiting supporters

↑ North direction (approx)

❶ B4137 Witton Lane
❷ B4140 Witton Road
❸ Trinity Road
❹ A4040 Aston Lane to A34 Walsall Road
❺ To Aston Expressway & M6
❻ Holte End
❼ Visitors' Car Park

*Left:*
Now firmly established in the England set-up, where his performances with the national team in Euro '96 were impressive, Gareth Southgate has also shown excellent form for Villa over the past season.

# BARNET

## Underhill Stadium, Barnet Lane, Barnet, Herts, EN5 2BE

**Tel No:** 0181 441 6932
**Advance Tickets Tel No:** 0181 441 6932
**Credit Card Bookings:** 0181 441 1677
**League:** 3rd Division
**Brief History:** Founded 1888 as Barnet Alston. Changed name to Barnet (1919). Former grounds: Queens Road & Totteridge Lane. Promoted to Football League 1991. Record attendance 11,026.
**(Total) Current capacity:** Approx. 4,000 (approx 1,800 seated)
**Visiting Supporters' Allocation:** Approx. 800 (50% seated)
**Club Colours:** Amber & Black striped shirts, black shorts.
**Nearest Railway Station:** New Barnet (High Barnet - Tube)

**Parking (Car):** Street Parking & High Barnet Station
**Parking (Coach/Bus):** As directed by Police
**Police Force and Tel No:** Metropolitan (0181) 200 2212
**Disabled Visitors' Facilities**
  **Wheelchairs:** Barnet Lane (Social Club end - few spaces)
  **Blind:** No special facility
**Anticipated Development(s):** There is nothing definite planned at this stage although there are rumours of a relocation. The temporary seating in the South Stand installed for the 1995/96 season will remain during 1996/97.

### KEY

**C** Club Offices
**S** Club Shop
**E** Entrance(s) for visiting supporters
**R** Refreshment bars for visiting supporters
**T** Toilets for visiting supporters

↑ North direction (approx)

❶ Barnet Lane
❷ Westcombe Drive
❸ A1000 Barnet Hill
❹ New Barnet BR Station (1 mile)
❺ To High Barnet Tube Station, M1 & M25

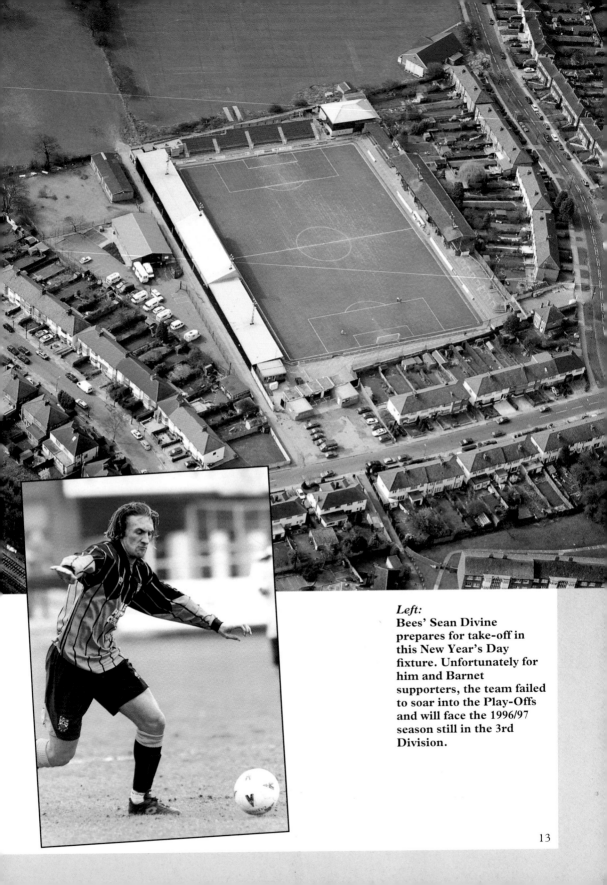

*Left:*
**Bees' Sean Divine prepares for take-off in this New Year's Day fixture. Unfortunately for him and Barnet supporters, the team failed to soar into the Play-Offs and will face the 1996/97 season still in the 3rd Division.**

13

# BARNSLEY

## Oakwell Ground, Grove Street, Barnsley, S71 1ET

**Tel No:** 01226 211211
**Advance Tickets Tel No:** 01226 211211
**League:** 1st Division
**Brief History:** Founded 1887 as Barnsley St Peter's, changed name to Barnsley in 1897. Former Ground: Doncaster Road, Worsboro Bridge until 1888. Record attendance 40,255.
**(Total) Current capacity:** 19,000 (all seated)
**Visiting Supporters' Allocation:** 4,322 (seating in North Stand, plus uncovered seating behind goal)
**Club Colours:** Red shirts, white shorts
**Nearest Railway Station:** Barnsley Exchange

**Parking (Car):** Queen's Ground car park
**Parking (Coach/Bus):** Queen's Ground car park
**Police Force and Tel No:** South Yorkshire (01226) 206161
**Disabled Visitors' Facilities**
  **Wheelchairs:** Purpose Built Disabled Stand
  **Blind:** Commentary available
**Anticipated Development(s):** With the completion of the West Stand, attention is now focused on the Spion Kop, although there are no definite plans as yet.

---

### KEY

**C** Club Offices
**S** Club Shop
**E** Entrance(s) for visiting supporters
**R** Refreshment bars for visiting supporters
**T** Toilets for visiting supporters

↑ North direction (approx)

❶ A628 Pontefract Road
❷ To Barnsley Exchange BR station and M1 Junction 37 (two miles)
❸ Queen's Ground Car Park

*Left:*
**One of the 1st Division's dark horses, Barnsley's form improved as the season progressed and the team found itself on the fringes of the chase for Play-Off spots towards the end of the season. Just missing out, supporters will no doubt better things of the club in 1996/97. Peter Shirtliff is featured here in an early 1995/96 fixture.**

# BIRMINGHAM CITY

## St Andrew's, St. Andrew's Street, Birmingham, B9 4NH

**Tel No:** 0121 772 0101
**Advance Tickets Tel No:** 0121 766 5743
**Advance Tickets Kop Ticket Office:** 0121 753 3408
**League:** 1st Division
**Brief History:** Founded 1875, as Small Heath Alliance. Changed to Small Heath in 1888, Birmingham in 1905, Birmingham City in 1945. Former Grounds: Arthur Street, Ladypool Road, Muntz Street, moved to St Andrew's in 1906. Record attendance 68,844.
**(Total) Current Capacity:** 25,000
**Visiting Supporters' Allocation:** 3,600
**Club Colours:** Blue shirts, White shorts

**Nearest Railway Station:** Birmingham New Street
**Parking (Car):** Street parking
**Parking (Coach/Bus):** Coventry Road
**Police Force and Tel No:** West Midlands (0121 772 1169)
**Disabled Visitors' Facilities**
  **Wheelchairs:** Remploy stand (St Andrew's Street), advanced notice required.
  **Blind:** No special facilities.
**Anticipated Development(s):** Nothing definite, but the next stage in any redevelopment will involve the Railway End.

### KEY
- **C** Club Offices
- **S** Club Shop
- **E** Entrance(s) for visiting supporters
- **R** Refreshment bars for visiting supporters
- **T** Toilets for visiting supporters

↑ North direction (approx)

- ❶ Car Park
- ❷ B4128 Cattell Road
- ❸ Tilton Road
- ❹ Garrison Lane
- ❺ To A4540 & A38 (M)
- ❻ To City Centre and New Street BR Station (1½ miles)

*Left:*
**Under the managership of the astute Barry Fry, much was expected from Gary Poole and the rest of the Birmingham City team. Unfortunately, the team failed to deliver and Fry ultimately paid the price for the lack of success.**

# BLACKBURN ROVERS

## Ewood Park, Blackburn, Lancashire, BB2 4JF

**Tel No:** 01254 698888
**Advance Tickets Tel No:** 01254 698888
(696767 Credit card line)
**League:** F.A. Premier
**Brief History:** Founded 1875. Former Grounds:
Oozebooth, Pleasington Cricket Ground,
Alexandra Meadows. Moved to Ewood Park in
1890. Founder members of Football League
(1888). Record attendance 61,783.
**(Total) Current Capacity:** 31,367 (all seated)
**Visiting Supporters' Allocation:** 3,800

**Club Colours:** Blue & white halved shirts, white
shorts
**Nearest Railway Station:** Blackburn
**Parking (Car):** Street parking
**Parking (Coach/Bus):** As directed by Police
**Police Force and Tel No:** Lancashire (01254
51212)
**Disabled Visitors' Facilities**
**Wheelchairs** : All sides of the ground
**Blind:** Commentary available.
**Anticipated Development(s):** None anticipated.

## KEY

**C** Club Offices
**S** Club Shop
**E** Entrance(s) for visiting supporters
**R** Refreshment bars for visiting supporters
**T** Toilets for visiting supporters

↑ North direction (approx)

❶ A666 Bolton Road
❷ Kidder Street
❸ Nuttall Street
❹ Town Centre & Blackburn Central BR Station (1½ miles)
❺ To Darwen and Bolton
❻ Car parking area for 500 cars
❼ Car Parks
❽ Top O'Croft Road

*Left:*
**After the triumph of the 1994/95 season, 1995/96 proved less successful for Graeme Le Saux and the rest of the Blackburn team. Le Saux spent much of the season injured, but with the departure of Alan Shearer for a world record £15 million, a great deal will be expected of him and his Rovers' team mates in 1996/97.**

# BLACKPOOL

## Bloomfield Road, Blackpool, Lancashire, FY1 6JJ

**Tel No:** 01253 404331

**Advance Tickets Tel No:** 01253 404331

**League:** 2nd Division

**Brief History:** Founded 1887, merged with 'South Shore' (1899). Former grounds: Raikes Hall (twice) and Athletic Grounds, Stanley Park. South Shore played at Cow Cap Lane, moved to Bloomfield Road in 1899. Record attendance 38,098

**(Total) Current Capacity:** 9,701 (2,987 seated)

**Visiting Supporters' Allocation:** 2,300 min.(none seated)

**Club Colours:** Tangerine shirts, tangerine shorts

**Nearest Railway Station:** Blackpool South

**Parking (Car):** At Ground & street parking (also behind West Stand - from M55)

**Parking (Coach/Bus):** Mecca car park (behind North End, (also behind West Stand - from M55)

**Police Force and Tel No:** Lancashire (01253 293933)

**Disabled Visitors' Facilities**
**Wheelchairs:** By players entrance
**Blind:** Commentary available

**Anticipated Development(s):** Planning permission is being sought for the construction of a new stadium. It is hoped that it will be operational by the start of the 1998/99 season.

### KEY

**C** Club Offices

**E** Entrance(s) for visiting supporters

**S** Club Shop

**R** Refreshment bars for visiting supporters

**T** Toilets for visiting supporters

⬆ North direction (approx)

❶ Car Parks
❷ To Blackpool South BR Station (1/2 mile) and M55 Junction 4
❸ Bloomfield Drive
❹ Central Drive
❺ Henry Street
❻ Blackpool Greyhound Stadium
❼ Blackpool Tower

*Left:*
For a long time it looked as though Blackpool would gain automatic promotion to the 1st Division. Mick Mellon and his team-mates were, however, pipped on the final day of the season by Oxford United and then capped an unhappy season by throwing away a two-goal advantage over Bradford City in the first round of the Play-Offs.

# BOLTON WANDERERS

## Burnden Park, Manchester Road, Bolton, BL3 2QR

**Tel No:** 01204 389200
**Advance Tickets Tel No:** 01204 521101
**League:** 1st Division
**Brief History:** Founded 1874 as Christ Church until 1877. Former Grounds: Several Fields, moved to Pikes Lane in 1880, moved to Burnden Park in 1895. Founder-members of Football League (1888). Record attendance 69,912.
**(Total) Current Capacity:** 20,800 (7,400 seated)
**Visiting Supporters' Allocation:** 4,650
**Club Colours:** White shirts, blue shorts
**Nearest Railway Station:** Bolton Trinity Street

**Parking (Car):** Rosehill car park, Manchester Road
**Parking (Coach/Bus):** Rosehill car park, Manchester Road
**Police Force and Tel No:** Greater Manchester (01204 522466)
**Disabled Visitors' Facilities**
  **Wheelchairs:** Manchester Road (few)
  **Blind:** No special facility
**Anticipated Development(s):** Work is in hand for the construction of a new 25,000 all-seater stadium at nearby Horwich. This will open for the 1997/98 season.

### KEY

**E** Entrance(s) for visiting supporters
**R** Refreshment bars for visiting supporters
**T** Toilets for visiting supporters

↑ North direction (approx)

❶ Car Parks
❷ B6536 Manchester Road
❸ A666 St Peter's Way
❹ Bolton Trinity Street BR Station (1/2 mile)
❺ To M61 Junction 3 (3 miles)
❻ Supermarket

*Left:*

**As prophesied by most of the pundits, Bolton Wanderers struggled through their season back in the top flight, and few were surprised by the team's immediate return to the 1st Division. The team, however, refused to succumb without a struggle and produced a number of stirring performances. One of the team's successes was striker Sasa Curcic.**

# A.F.C. BOURNEMOUTH

## Dean Court, Bournemouth, Dorset BH7 7AF

**Tel No:** 01202 395381
**Advance Tickets Tel No:** 01202 395381
**League:** 2nd Division
**Brief History:** Founded 1890 as Boscombe St. John's, changed to Boscombe (1899), Bournemouth & Boscombe Athletic (1923) and A.F.C. Bournemouth (1971). Former grounds: Kings Park (twice) and Castlemain Road, Pokesdown. Moved to Dean Court in 1910. Record attendance 28,799.
**(Total) Current Capacity:** 11,000 (3,080 seated)
**Visiting Supporters' Allocation:** 2,770 (150 Seated Family Stand only).
**Club Colours:** Red/Black and white pinstripe shirts, white shorts.

**Nearest Railway Station:** Bournemouth
**Parking (Car):** Large car park adjacent ground
**Parking (Coach/Bus):** Large car park adjacent ground
**Police Force and Tel No:** Dorset (01202) 552099
**Disabled Visitors' Facilities**
  **Wheelchairs:** South Stand (prior arrangement)
  **Blind:** No special facility
**Anticipated Development(s):** Planning permission has been granted for the construction of a 12,000 all-seater stadium at Dean Court. It is hoped that work will start during 1996.

### KEY

**C** Club Offices
**S** Club Shop
**E** Entrance(s) for visiting supporters
**R** Refreshment bars for visiting supporters
**T** Toilets for visiting supporters

↑ North direction (approx)

❶ Car Park
❷ A338 Wessex Way
❸ To Bournemouth BR Station (1½ miles)
❹ To A31 & M27

*Left:*
**The home team's Jason Brissett is pictured during the Cherries 2nd Division encounter with Shrewsbury Town at Dean Court on 2 January 1996.**

# BRADFORD CITY

## The Pulse Stadium, Valley Parade, Bradford, BD8 7DY

**Tel No:** 01274 773355
**Advance Tickets Tel No:** 01274 773355
**League:** 1st Division
**Brief History:** Founded 1903 (formerly Manningham Northern Union Rugby Club founded in 1876). Continued use of Valley Parade, joined 2nd Division on re-formation. Record attendance 39,146.
**(Total) Current Capacity:** 13,800 (6,666 seated)
**Visiting Supporters' Allocation:** 1,840 (all seated)
**Club Colours:** Claret & amber shirts, black shorts

**Nearest Railway Station:** Bradford Forster Square
**Parking (Car):** Street parking and car parks
**Parking (Coach/Bus):** As directed by Police
**Police Force and Tel No:** West Yorkshire (01274 723422)
**Disabled Visitors' Facilities**
  **Wheelchairs:** Sunwin (ex-N&P) Stand
  **Blind:** No special facility
**Anticipated Development(s):** The familiar Midland Road Terrace will be replaced during the summer of 1996 by a new Midland Road Stand.

---

*KEY*

**C** Club Offices
**E** Entrance(s) for visiting supporters

⬆ North direction (approx)

❶ Midland Road
❷ Valley Parade
❸ A650 Manningham Lane
❹ To City Centre, Forster Square and Interchange BR Stations M606 &M62
❺ To Keighley
❻ Car Parks

*Right:*
**The popular Ian Ormondroyd returned to Valley Parade during the 1995 close season from Leicester City. He played an important role in City's successful campaign, culminating in the club's first-ever appearance at Wembley and the triumph of victory in the 2nd Division Play-Off final.**

# BRENTFORD

## Griffin Park, Braemar Road, Brentford, Middlesex, TW8 0NT

**Tel No:** 0181 847 2511
**Advance Tickets Tel No:** 0181 847 2511
**League:** 2nd Division
**Brief History:** Founded 1889. Former Grounds: Clifden House Ground, Benn's Field (Little Ealing), Shotters Field, Cross Roads, Boston Park Cricket Ground, moved to Griffin Park in 1904. Founder-members Third Division (1920). Record attendance 39,626.
**(Total) Current Capacity:** 12,922 (9,079 seated)
**Visiting Supporters' Allocation:** 2,263 (636 seated)

**Club Colours:** Red & White striped shirts, black shorts
**Nearest Railway Station:** Brentford Central, South Ealing (tube)
**Parking (Car):** Street parking (restricted)
**Parking (Coach/Bus):** Layton Road car park
**Police Force and Tel No:** Metropolitan (0181 577 1212)
**Disabled Visitors' Facilities**
  **Wheelchairs:** Braemar Road
  **Blind:** Commentary available

**KEY**

**C** Club Offices
**S** Club Shop
**E** Entrance(s) for visiting supporters
**R** Refreshment bars for visiting supporters
**T** Toilets for visiting supporters

↑ North direction (approx)

❶ Ealing Road
❷ Braemar Road
❸ Brook Road South
❹ To M4 (¼ mile) & South Ealing Tube Station (1 mile)
❺ To Brentford Central BR Station
❻ To A315 High Street & Kew Bridge

**Left:**
Perhaps it was the after effects of the club's shock defeat at the end of the 1994/95 Play-Off Final, but the 1995/96 season was not one of the Bees' most successful. A disastrous start saw the team hovering in and around the relegation places, but a late season run saw mid-table safety by the end. No doubt fans will be expecting a great deal more from Denny Mundee and the rest of the team come 1996/97.

# BRIGHTON & HOVE ALBION

## Goldstone Ground, Newtown Road, Hove, Sussex, BN3 7DE

**Tel No:** 01273 778855
**Advance Tickets Tel No:** 01273 778855
**League:** 3rd Division
**Brief History:** Founded 1900 as Brighton and Hove Rangers, changed to Brighton and Hove Albion in 1902. Former Grounds: Home Farm (Withdean) and County Ground, moved to Goldstone Ground in 1902. Founder members Third Division (1920). Record attendance 36,747.
**(Total) Current Capacity:** Approx 13,500
**Visiting Supporters' Allocation:** 3,255 (738 seated)
**Club Colours:** Blue & white striped shirts, blue shorts
**Nearest Railway Station:** Hove

**Parking (Car):** Greyhound Stadium and street parking
**Parking (Coach/Bus):** Conway Street
**Police Force and Tel No:** Sussex (01273 778922)
**Disabled Visitors' Facilities**
  **Wheelchairs:** Newtown Road (South West corner)
  **Blind:** Commentary available
**Anticipated Development(s):** Having sold the Goldstone Ground and having failed to arrange a groundshare with Portsmouth, Brighton was in danger of folding at the end of the 1995/96 season. However, the club will remain at the Goldstone for a further season; thereafter its position is uncertain.

### KEY

**C** Club Offices
**S** Club Shop
**E** Entrance(s) for visiting supporters
**R** Refreshment bars for visiting supporters
**T** Toilets for visiting supporters

⬆ North direction (approx)

❶ A27 Old Shoreham Road
❷ Nevill Road
❸ To A2038 & A23
❹ Goldstone Lane
❺ Newtown Road
❻ Greyhound Stadium
❼ Hove BR Station

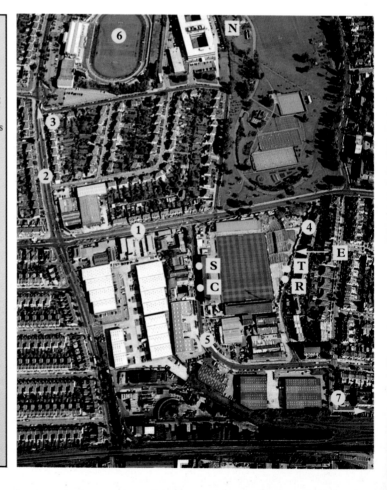

# BRISTOL CITY

## Ashton Gate, Winterstoke Road, Ashton Road, Bristol, BS3 2EJ

**Tel No:** 0117 9632812
**Advance Tickets Tel No:** 0117 9632812
**League:** 2nd Division
**Brief History:** Founded 1894 as Bristol South End changed to Bristol City in 1897. Former Ground: St. John's Lane, Bedminster, moved to Ashton Gate in 1904. Record attendance 43,335
**(Total) Current Capacity:** 21,000 (all seated)
**Visiting supporters' Allocation:** 2,500 (all seated)
**Club Colours:** Red shirts, white shorts

**Nearest Railway Station:** Bristol Temple Meads
**Parking (Car):** Street parking
**Parking (Coach/Bus):** Marsh Road
**Police Force and Tel No:** Avon/Somerset (0117 9277777)
**Disabled Visitors' Facilities**
　**Wheelchairs:** Advanced notice not required
　**Blind:** Commentary available
**Anticipated Development(s):** None anticipated.

| KEY | |
|---|---|
| **C** | Club Offices |
| **S** | Club Shop |
| **E** | Entrance(s) for visiting supporters |

↑ North direction (approx)

❶ A370 Ashton Road
❷ A3209 Winterstoke Road
❸ To Temple Meads Station (1½ miles)
❹ To City Centre, A4, M32 & M4

*Left:*
**Martin Kuhl anticipates
the arrival of the ball; no
doubt City fans expect the
new season to bring the
team threatening the top,
rather than the bottom, of
the 2nd Division.**

33

# BRISTOL ROVERS

## The Memorial Ground, Filton Avenue, Horfield, Bristol BS7 0AQ

(**Office:** 199, Two Mile Hill Road, Kingswood, Bristol, BS15 1AZ)

**Tel No:** 0117 986 9999

**Advance Tickets Tel No:** 0117 986 9999

**League:** 2nd Division

**Brief History:** Founded 1883 as Black Arabs, changed to Eastville Rovers (1884), Bristol Eastville Rovers (1896) and Bristol Rovers in 1897. Former Grounds: Purdown, Three Acres, The Downs (Horfield), Ridgeway, Bristol Stadium (Eastville) moved to Twerton Park in 1986. Record attendance (at Eastville) 38,472. (At Twerton Park) 9,813.

(**Total**) **Current Capacity:** 11,500 (2,000 seated)

**Visiting Supporters' Allocation:** c1,500 (location to be confirmed)

**Club Colours:** Blue & white quartered shirts, white shorts

**Nearest Railway Station:** Filton or Stapleton Road

**Parking (Car):** Limited parking at the ground; some on street parking in the vicinity.

**Police Force and Telephone Number:** Avon/Somerset (0117 927 7777)

**Disabled Visitors' Facilities**
  **Wheelchairs:** A number of places will be provided in the new West Stand.
  **Blind:** Not currently available but this may change during the course of the season.

**Anticipated Development(s):** The club still hopes to construct an all-seater stadium in Bristol, but its plans have as yet come to nothing.

**KEY**

**C** Rugby Club offices

↑ North direction (approx)

❶ Filton Avenue
❷ Gloucester Road
❸ Muller Road
❹ To Bristol city centre (2.5 miles) and BR Temple Meads station (3 miles)
❺ Downer Road
❻ Ashley Down Road
❼ To M32 J2 (1.5 miles)
❽ Strathmore Road
❾ To Filton (1.5 miles)
❿ Centenary Stand
⓫ Car Park

*Left:*
After several years of 'exile' in neighbouring Bath, the 1996/97 season brings Rovers back to Bristol in the shape of a ground-sharing scheme with the Bristol rugby club. Rovers' Ian Wright is captured in action during the game against Notts County on 9 April 1996.

# BURNLEY

## Turf Moor, Brunshaw Road, Burnley, Lancs, BB10 4BX

**Tel No:** 01282 700000
**Advance Tickets Tel No:** 01282 700010
**League:** 2nd Division
**Brief History:** Founded 1882, Burnley Rovers (Rugby Club) combined with another Rugby Club, changed to soccer and name to Burnley. Moved from Calder Vale to Turf Moor in 1882. Founder-members Football League (1888). Record attendance 54,775.
**(Total) Current Capacity:** 15,601 (all seated)
**Visiting Supporters' Allocation:** 810 (all seated)
**Club Colours:** Claret with blue sleeved shirts, white shorts

**Nearest Railway Station:** Burnley Central
**Parking (Car):** Church Street and Fulledge Rec. (car parks)
**Parking (Coach/Bus):** As directed by Police
**Police Force and Tel No:** Lancashire (01282 425001)
**Disabled Visitors' Facilities**
   **Wheelchairs:** Bob Lord Stand – Pre-match applications
   **Blind:** Headsets provided with commentary.
**Anticipated Development(s):** Work is in hand converting the Bee Hole Terrace into a 4,840 stand. Once this is completed, the club hopes to redevelop the Endsleigh Stand.

*KEY*
**C** Club Offices
**E** Entrance(s) for visiting supporters

↑ North direction (approx)

❶ Brunshaw Road
❷ Belvedere Road
❸ Burnley Central BR Station (¹/₂ mile)
❹ Cricket Ground

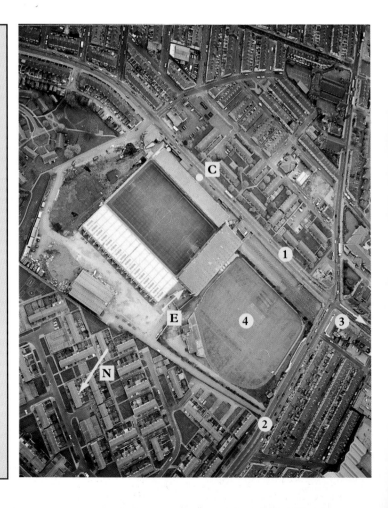

36

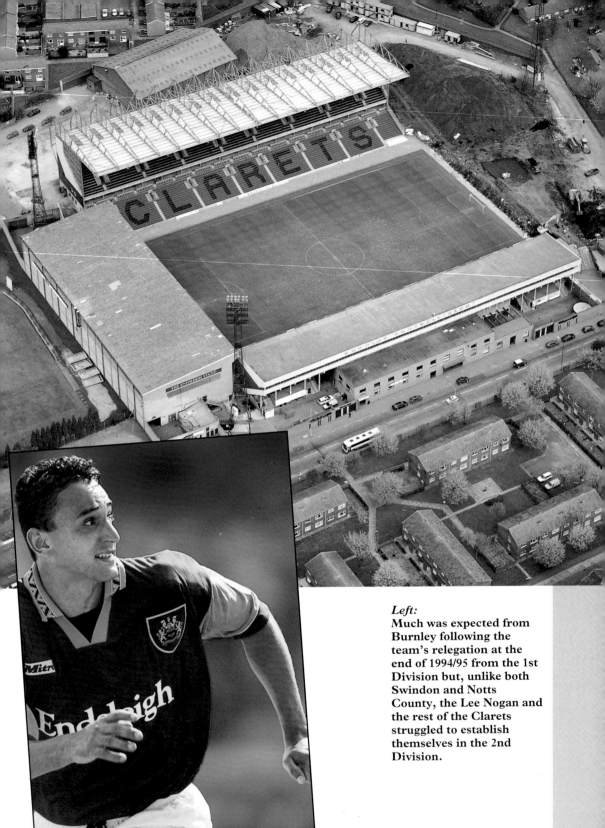

*Left:*
**Much was expected from Burnley following the team's relegation at the end of 1994/95 from the 1st Division but, unlike both Swindon and Notts County, the Lee Nogan and the rest of the Clarets struggled to establish themselves in the 2nd Division.**

# BURY

## Gigg Lane, Bury, Lancashire, BL9 9HR

**Tel No:** 0161 764 4881
**Advance Tickets Tel No:** 0161 764 4881
**League:** 2nd Division
**Brief History:** Founded 1885, no former names or former grounds. Record attendance 35,000
**(Total) Current Capacity:** 11,500 (8,600 seated)
**Visiting Supporters' Allocation:** 2,500 (all seated)
**Club Colours:** White shirts, royal blue shorts
**Nearest Railway Station:** Bury Interchange

**Parking (Car):** Street parking
**Parking (Coach/Bus):** As directed by Police
**Police Force and Tel No:** Greater Manchester (0161 872 5050)
**Disabled Visitors' Facilities**
  **Wheelchairs:** South Stand
  **Blind:** Radio commentary (Press box)
**Anticipated Development(s):** Following the completion of the South Stand, the club will next turn to the Cemetery End with a planned completion date of 1997.

*KEY*

**C** Club Offices
**S** Club Shop
**E** Entrance(s) for visiting supporters
**R** Refreshment bars for visiting supporters
**T** Toilets for visiting supporters

⬆ North direction (approx)

❶ Car Park
❷ Gigg Lane
❸ A56 Manchester Road
❹ Town Centre & Bury Interchange (Metrolink) (³/₄ mile)

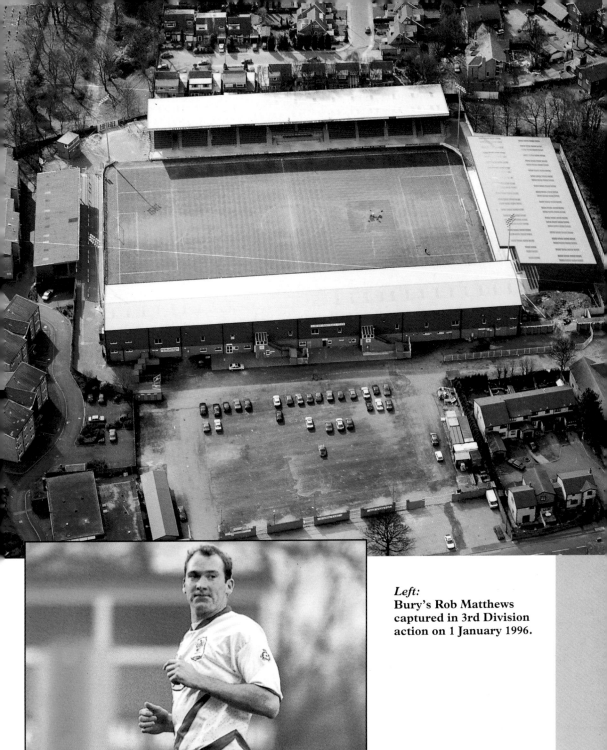

*Left:*
**Bury's Rob Matthews captured in 3rd Division action on 1 January 1996.**

# CAMBRIDGE UNITED

## Abbey Stadium, Newmarket Road, Cambridge, CB5 8LN

**Tel No:** 01223 566500
**Advance Tickets Tel No:** 01223 566500
**League:** 3rd Division
**Brief History:** Founded 1913 as Abbey United, changed to Cambridge United in 1949. Former Grounds: Midsummer Common, Stourbridge Common, Station Farm Barnwell (The Celery Trenches) & Parker's Piece, moved to Abbey Stadium in 1933. Record attendance 14,000.
**(Total) Current Capacity:** 9,667 (3,410 seated)
**Visiting Supporters' Allocation:** 2,216 (366 seated)
**Club Colours:** Amber and black shirts, black shorts

**Nearest Railway Station:** Cambridge (2 miles)
**Parking (Car):** Coldhams Common
**Parking (Coach/Bus):** Coldhams Common
**Police Force and Tel No:** Cambridge (01223 358966)
**Disabled Visitors' Facilities**
  **Wheelchairs:** Limited number that should be pre-booked
  **Blind:** No special facility
**Anticipated Development(s):** Possible future relocation, but nothing definite.

*KEY*
**C** Club Offices
**S** Club Shop
**E** Entrance(s) for visiting supporters
**R** Refreshment bars for visiting supporters
**T** Toilets for visiting supporters

↑ North direction (approx)

❶ A1134 Newmarket Road
❷ To A11 & Newmarket
❸ To City Centre, Cambridge BR Station (2 miles) & M11
❹ Whitehill Road

*Left:*
**Although United's David Thompson appears to be seeking heavenly inspiration in this pre-season friendly against Coventry City in July 1995, the team had their feet firmly rooted to the ground in the 3rd Division and never looked like reclaiming the 2nd Division spot they had surrendered the previous year.**

# CARDIFF CITY

## Ninian Park, Sloper Road, Cardiff, CF1 8SX

**Tel No:** 01222 398636
**Advance Tickets Tel No:** 01222 398636
**League:** 3rd Division
**Brief History:** Founded 1899. Former Grounds: Riverside Cricket Club, Roath, Sophia Gardens, Cardiff Arms Park & The Harlequins Rugby Ground, moved to Ninian Park in 1910. Ground record attendance 61,566 (Wales v. England, 1961)
**(Total) Current Capacity:** 13,695 (11,371 seated)
**Visiting Supporters' Allocation:** 3,263
**Club Colours:** Blue shirts, blue shorts
**Nearest Railway Station:** Ninian Park (adjacent) (Cardiff Central 1 mile)

**Parking (Car):** Opposite Ground, no street parking around ground
**Parking (Coach/Bus):** Sloper Road
**Police Force and Tel No:** South Wales (01222 222111)
**Disabled Visitors' Facilities**
  **Wheelchairs:** Corner Canton Stand/Popular Bank (covered)
  **Blind:** No special facility
**Anticipated Development(s):** Nothing definite planned.

### KEY

**C** Club Offices
**E** Entrance(s) for visiting supporters
**R** Refreshment bars for visiting supporters
**T** Toilets for visiting supporters (Terrace only, when used)

↑ North direction (approx)

❶ Sloper Road
❷ B4267 Leckwith Road
❸ Car Park
❹ To A4232 & M4 Junction 33 (8 miles)
❺ Ninian Park Road
❻ To City Centre & Cardiff Central BR Station (1 mile)
❼ To A48 Western Avenue, A48M, and M4 Junctions 32 and 29
❽ Ninian Park BR station

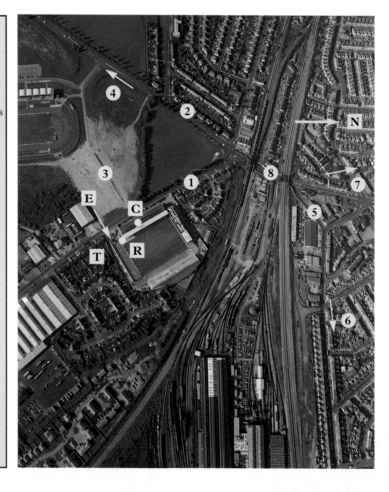

*Left:*
Another team that failed to shine following relegation, Cardiff City at least have the prospect of a derby against Swansea to brighten up their 1996/97 season. City's Ian Rogerson seems to be endeavouring to hypnotise the ball.

# CARLISLE UNITED

## Brunton Park, Warwick Road, Carlisle, CA1 1LL

**Tel No:** 01228 26237
**Advance Tickets Tel No:** 01228 26237
**League:** 3rd Division
**Brief History:** Founded 1904 as Carlisle United (previously named Shaddongate United). Former Grounds: Millholme Bank and Devonshire Park, moved to Brunton Park in 1909. Record attendance 27,500.
**(Total) Current capacity:** 16,650 (9,162 seated)
**Visiting Supporters' Allocation:** 1,445 (430 seated)
**Club Colours:** Royal blue shirts, white shorts
**Nearest Railway Station:** Carlisle Citadel

**Parking (Car):** Rear of ground
**Parking (Coach/Bus):** St. Aiden's Road car park
**Police Force and Tel No:** Cumbria (01228 28191)
**Disabled Visitors' Facilities**
  **Wheelchairs:** Front of Main Stand (prior arrangement)
  **Blind:** No special facilities
**Anticipated Development(s):** Long term plans for a 28,000 all-seater stadium, but nothing concrete planned after completion of the new East Stand.

| KEY | |
| --- | --- |
| **C** | Club Offices |
| **E** | Entrance(s) for visiting supporters |
| **R** | Refreshment bars for visiting supporters |
| **T** | Toilets for visiting supporters |

⬆ North direction (approx)

❶ A69 Warwick Road
❷ To M6 Junction 43
❸ Carlisle Citadel BR Station (1 mile)
❹ Greystone Road
❺ Car Park

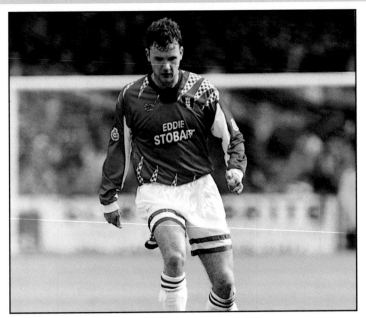

*Left:*
If a week is a long time in politics then a year is an eternity in football. At the end of the 1994/95 season United celebrated winning the 3rd Division title in style and Michael Knighton's avowed intention of getting the club to the Premiership within 10 years looked on course. A disastrous 1995/96, however, saw United relegated after just one season in the 2nd Division. Jamie Robinson is seen in the league encounter against Bristol City.

# CHARLTON ATHLETIC

## The Valley, Floyd Road, Charlton, London, SE7 8BL

**Tel No:** 0181 333 4000
**Advance Tickets Tel No:** 0181 333 4010
**League:** 1st Division
**Brief History:** Founded 1905. Former grounds: Siemens Meadows, Woolwich Common, Pound Park, Angerstein Athletic Ground, The Mount Catford, Selhurst Park (Crystal Palace FC), Boleyn Ground (West Ham United FC), The Valley (1919-1923, 1924-85, 1992- ). Founder Members 3rd Division South. Record attendance 75,031.
**(Total) Current Capacity:** 14,986 all seated

**Visiting Supporters' Allocation:** 3,073 (all seated)
**Club Colours:** Red shirts, white shorts
**Nearest Railway Station:** Charlton
**Parking (Car):** Street parking
**Parking (Coach/Bus):** As directed by Police
**Police Force and Tel No:** Metropolitan (0181 853 8212)
**Disabled Visitors' Facilities**
  **Wheelchairs:** East/West Stands
  **Blind:** Commentary, 12 spaces.

**KEY**

**C** Club Offices
**E** Entrance(s) for visiting supporters

↑ North direction (approx)

❶ Harvey Gardens
❷ A206 Woolwich Road
❸ Valley Grove
❹ Floyd Road
❺ Charlton BR Station
❻ River Thames
❼ Thames Barrier

*Left:*
The impressive form of Carl Leaburn was one factor in Charlton Athletic's successful climb to the Play-Off places in the 1st Division. However, defeat in the first round by Crystal Palace consigned the Addicks to a further season in the 1st Division.

# CHELSEA

## Stamford Bridge, Fulham Road, London, SW6 1HS

**Tel No:** 0171 385 5545
**Advance Tickets Tel No:** 0171 385 5545
**League:** F.A. Premier
**Brief History:** Founded 1905. Admitted to Football League (2nd Division) on formation. Stamford Bridge venue for F.A. Cup Finals 1919-1922. Record attendance 82,905.
**(Total) Current capacity:** 30,688 (all seated)
**Visiting Supporters' Allocation:** Approx. 1,750
**Club Colours:** Blue shirts, blue shorts
**Nearest Railway Station:** Fulham Broadway

**Parking (Car):** Street parking
**Parking (Coach/Bus):** As directed by Police
**Police Force and Tel No:** Metropolitan (0171 385 1212)
**Disabled Visitors' Facilities**
  **Wheelchairs:** East Stand
  **Blind:** No special facility
**Anticipated Development(s):** The 2,200-seat link between the North and West stands should open for the 1996/97 season. Further plans uncertain.

### KEY
**C** Club Offices
**S** Club Shop
**E** Entrance(s) for visiting supporters

↑ North direction (approx)

❶ A308 Fulham Road
❷ Central London
❸ Fulham Broadway Tube Station

*Left:*
**Few of the international imports were as successful as the stylish Ruud Gullit. With Glenn Hoddle's appointment to the position of England coach, the 1996/97 season promises new challenges for the great Dutch player as he combines the role of Chelsea manager with his playing commitments.**

# CHESTER CITY

## The Deva Stadium, Bumpers Lane, Chester

**Tel No:** 01244 371376
**Advance Tickets Tel No:** 01244 371376
**Commercial:** 01244 390243
**League:** 3rd Division
**Brief History:** Founded 1884 from amalgamation of Chester Wanderers and Chester Rovers. Former Grounds: Faulkner Street, Lightfoot Street, Whipcord Lane, Sealand Road, Moss Rose (Macclesfield Town F.C.), moved to Deva Stadium in 1992. Record attendance (Sealand Road) 20,500.
**(Total) Current Capacity:** 6,000 (3,408 seated)

**Visiting Supporters' Allocation:** 1,933 max (seated 637 max.)
**Club Colours:** Blue/White striped shirts, White shorts
**Nearest Railway Station:** Chester (3 miles)
**Parking (Car):** Car park at ground
**Parking (Coach/Bus):** Car park at ground
**Police Force and Tel No:** Cheshire (01244 350222)
**Disabled Visitors' Facilities**
 **Wheelchairs:** West and East Stand
 **Blind:** Facility available

**KEY**

**C** Club Offices
**S** Club Shop
**E** Entrance(s) for visiting supporters
**R** Refreshment bars for visiting supporters
**T** Toilets for visiting supporters

↑ North direction (approx)

❶ Bumpers Lane
❷ To City Centre and Chester BR Station (1½ miles)
❸ Car Park

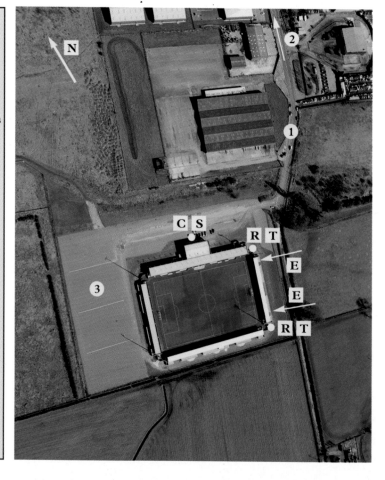

*Left:*
**Former England striker Cyrille Regis is now gracing the Deva Stadium in the twilight years of his playing career.**

# CHESTERFIELD

## Recreation Ground, Saltergate, Chesterfield, S40 4SX

**Tel No:** 01246 209765
**Advance Tickets Tel No:** 01246 209765
**League:** 2nd Division
**Brief History:** Founded 1866. Former Ground: Spital Vale. Formerly named Chesterfield Town. Record attendance 30,968
**(Total) Current Capacity:** 8,954 (2,674 Seated)
**Visiting Supporters' Allocation:** 3,185
**Club Colours:** Blue shirts, white shorts
**Nearest Railway Station:** Chesterfield

**Parking (Car):** Saltergate car park, street parking
**Parking (Coach/Bus):** As directed by Police
**Police Force and Tel No:** Derbyshire (01246 220100)
**Disabled Visitors' Facilities**
  **Wheelchairs:** Saltergate Stand
  **Blind:** No special facility
**Anticipated Development(s):** Plans in hand for a move to a new all-seater stadium for the start of the 1997/98 season.

### KEY

**C** Club Offices
**S** Club Shop
**E** Entrance(s) for visiting supporters
**R** Refreshment bars for visiting supporters
**T** Toilets for visiting supporters

↑ North direction (approx)

❶ Saltergate
❷ Cross Street
❸ St Margaret's Drive
❹ A632 West Bars
❺ To A617 & M1 Junction 29

*Left:*
**A promising first season back in the 2nd Division saw Chesterfield just miss out at the end on a Play-Off spot. Phil Robinson gets the ball away from under the feet of Swindon's Kevin Horlock during the league encounter on 23 April 1996.**

# COLCHESTER UNITED

## Layer Road Ground, Colchester, CO2 7JJ

**Tel No:** 01206 574042
**Advance Tickets Tel No:** 01206 574042
**League:** 3rd Division
**Brief History:** Founded 1937, joined Football League 1950, relegated 1990, promoted 1992. Record attendance 19,072.
**(Total) Current Capacity:** 7,190 (1,147 Seated)
**Visiting Supporters' Allocation:** 1,342
**Club Colours:** Royal Blue and white shirts, White shorts

**Nearest Railway Station:** Colchester Town
**Parking (Car):** Street parking
**Parking (Coach/Bus):** Boadicea Way
**Police Force and Tel No:** Essex (01206 762212)
**Disabled Visitor' Facilities**
  **Wheelchairs:** Space for six in front of terrace (next to Main Stand)
  **Blind:** Space for 3 blind persons and 3 guiders.
**Anticipated Development(s):** Plans are in hand for the redevelopment of the Rainsborowe Road End.

### KEY
**C** Club Offices
**S** Club Shop
**E** Entrance(s) for visiting supporters
**R** Refreshment bars for visiting supporters
**T** Toilets for visiting supporters

↑ North direction (approx)

❶ B1026 Layer Road
❷ Town Centre & Colchester Town BR Station (2 miles)
❸ Main Stand
❹ Popular Side

*Left:*
**Veteran striker Tony Adcock was one factor in a successful 1995/96 season for Colchester United, which saw the team reach the Play-Offs. Unfortunately defeat consigned United to another season of 3rd Division football.**

# COVENTRY CITY

## Highfield Stadium, King Richard Street, Coventry CV2 4FW.

**Tel No:** 01203 234000
**Advance Tickets Tel No:** 01203 225545
**League:** F.A. Premier
**Brief History:** Founded 1883 as Singers F.C., changed name to Coventry City in 1898. Former grounds; Dowell's Field, Stoke Road Ground, moved to Highfield Road in 1899. Record attendance, 51,455.
**(Total) Current Capacity:** 23,672 all seated
**Visiting Supporters' Allocation:** 4,154 all seated

**Club Colours:** Sky blue shirts, sky blue shorts.
**Nearest Railway Station:** Coventry.
**Parking (Car):** Street parking
**Parking (Coach/Bus):** Gosford Green Coach Park.
**Police Force and Tel No:** West Midlands (01203 539010)
**Disabled Visitors' Facilities**
  **Wheelchairs:** Clock Stand and East Stand
  **Blind:** Clock Stand (booking necessary)

### KEY
**C** Club Offices
**S** Club Shop
**E** Entrance(s) for visiting supporters
**R** Refreshment bars for visiting supporters
**T** Toilets for visiting supporters

↑ North direction (approx)

❶ Swan Lane
❷ A4600 Walsgrave Road
❸ Thackhall Street
❹ Coventry BR Station (1 mile)
❺ To M6 Junction 2 and M69
❻ To M45 Junction 1
❼ Gosford Green Coach Park

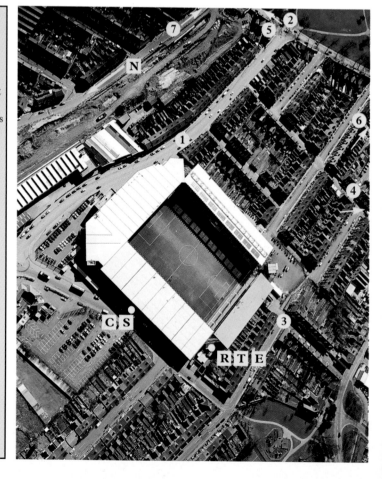

*Left:*
The ongoing Coventry escape story continued in the 1995/96 season, with the Sky Blues, now under the managership of Ron Atkinson, once again defying the pundits and maintaining their position in the FA Carling Premiership. One factor in their survival was the goal scoring of Dion Dublin.

# CREWE ALEXANDRA

## Gresty Road Ground, Crewe, Cheshire, CW2 6EB

**Tel No:** 01270 213014

**Advance Tickets Tel No:** 01270 213014

**League:** 2nd Division

**Brief History:** Founded 1877. Former Grounds;
Alexandra Recreation ground (Nantwich
Road), Earle Street Cricket Ground, Edleston
Road, Old Sheds Fields, Gresty Road
(Adjacent to current Ground), moved to
current Ground in 1906. Founder members of
2nd Division (1892) until 1896. Founder
members of 3rd Division North (1921). Record
attendance 20,000.

**(Total) Current Capacity:** 5,800 (4,700 seated)

**Visiting Supporters' Allocation:** 1,000

**Club Colours:** Red Shirts, White Shorts.

**Nearest Railway Station:** Crewe.

**Parking (Car):** Car Park near Ground

**Parking (Coach/Bus):** Car Park near Ground

**Police Force and Tel No:** Cheshire (01270
500222)

**Disabled Visitors' Facilities**
**Wheelchairs:** In visitors stand
**Blind:** Commentary available

*KEY*
- **C** Club Offices
- **S** Club Shop
- **E** Entrance(s) for visiting supporters
- **R** Refreshment bars for visiting supporters
- **T** Toilets for visiting supporters

⬆ North direction (approx)

- ❶ Crewe BR Station
- ❷ Car Park
- ❸ Gresty Road
- ❹ A534 Nantwich Road
- ❺ A5020 to M6 Junction 16
- ❻ To M6 Junction 17

Another frustrating season for Crewe Alexandra saw the team challenging for automatic promotion from the 2nd Division before a late loss of form saw them lose in the Play-Offs to Notts County. On 9 April 1996, however, Gareth Whalley looks as though he is sprinting towards the 1st Division in the league clash against eventual champions, Swindon Town.

# CRYSTAL PALACE

## Selhurst Park, London, SE25 6PY

**Tel No:** 0181 768 6000
**Advance Tickets Tel No:** 0181 768 6000
**League:** 1st Division
**Brief History:** Founded 1905. Former Grounds: The Crystal Palace (F.A. Cup Finals venue), London County Athletic Ground (Herne Hill), The Nest (Croydon Common Athletic Ground), moved to Selhurst Park in 1924. Founder members 3rd Division (1920). Record attendance 51,482.
**(Total) Current Capacity:** 26,400 all seated
**Visiting Supporters' Allocation:** Approx 2,500
**Club Colours:** Red with blue striped shirts, red shorts

**Nearest Railway Station:** Selhurst, Norwood Junction & Thornton Heath
**Parking (Car):** Street parking & Sainsbury's car park
**Parking (Coach/Bus):** Thornton Heath
**Police Force and Tel No:** Metropolitan (0181 653 8568)
**Disabled Visitors' Facilities**
  **Wheelchairs:** Arthur Wait and Holmesdale Stands
  **Blind:** Commentary available
**Anticipated Development(s):** Nothing confirmed following completion of Holmesdale Road stand.

---

**KEY**
**C** Club Offices
**S** Club Shop
**E** Entrance(s) for visiting supporters
**T** Toilets for visiting supporters

↑ North direction (approx)

❶ Whitehorse Lane
❷ Park Road
❸ A213 Selhurst Road
❹ Selhurst BR Station (1/2 mile)
❺ Norwood Junction BR Station (1/4 mile)
❻ Thornton Heath BR Station (1/2 mile)
❼ Car Park (Sainsbury's)

*Left:*
Under the leadership of Dave Bassett, the Eagles soared up the 1st Division table and for a period seemed as though they would be assured of an automatic promotion place. One of the team's most influential players was veteran Ray Houghton. Unfortunately, a season which had promised an immediate return to the top flight was thwarted by Leicester City in the 1st Division Play-Off final.

# DARLINGTON

## Feethams Ground, Darlington, DL1 5JB

**Tel No:** 01325 465097
**Advance Tickets Tel No:** 01325 465097
**League:** 3rd Division
**Brief History:** Founded 1883. Founder Members of 3rd Division North (1921), Relegated from 4th Division (1989). Promoted from GM Vauxhall Conference in 1990. Record attendance 21,023.
**(Total) Current Capacity:** 7,046 (1,120 seated)
**Visiting Supporters' Allocation:** 1,030 (200 seated)
**Club Colours:** White and Black Shirts, Black Shorts.
**Nearest Railway Station:** Darlington

**Parking (Car):** Street parking
**Parking (Coach/Bus):** As directed by Police
**Police Force and Tel No:** Durham (01325 467681)
**Disabled Visitors' Facilities**
  **Wheelchairs:** East Stand (free entrance)
  **Blind:** By prior arrangement
**Anticipated Development(s):** After toying with the idea of a move to an out of town site, the club has decided to upgrade the existing ground. Planning permission has just been granted and it is expected that work will start in September 1996.

*KEY*
- **C** Club Offices
- **S** Club Shop
- **E** Entrance(s) for visiting supporters
- **R** Refreshment bars for visiting supporters
- **T** Toilets for visiting supporters

↑ North direction (approx)

❶ Polam Lane
❷ Victoria Embankment
❸ Feethams Cricket Ground
❹ Victoria Road
❺ Darlington BR Station (¼ mile)
❻ To A1 (M)

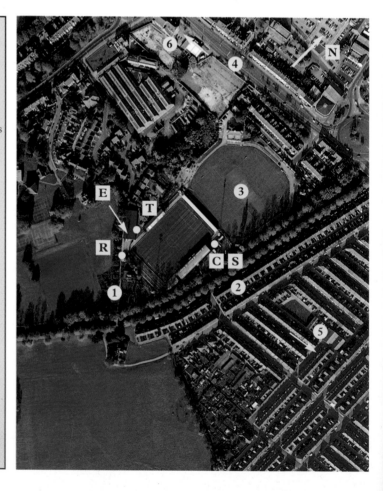

*Left:*
A promising season for the Quakers saw the team finish in the Play-Offs, where they were eventually defeated by Plymouth Argyle in the Final at Wembley. Pictured during the match on 25 May 1996, Gary Bannister battles with Argyle's striker Adrian Littlejohn.

# DERBY COUNTY

## Baseball Ground, Shaftesbury Crescent, Derby, DE3 8NB

**Tel No:** 01332 340105
**Advance Tickets Tel No:** 01332 340105
**League:** F.A. Premier
**Brief History:** Founded 1884. Former Ground: The Racecourse Ground, moved to Baseball Ground in 1894. Founder-members of the Football League (1888). Record attendance 41,826.
**(Total) Current Capacity:** 17,665 (all seated)
**Club Colours:** White shirts, black shorts
**Nearest Railway Station:** Derby Midland and Ramsline Halt (specials)

**Parking (Car):** Several car parks
**Parking (Coach/Bus):** Russel Street
**Police Force and Tel No:** Derbyshire (01332 290100)
**Disabled Visitors' Facilities**
    **Wheelchairs:** Normanton Stand
    **Blind:** Commentary available
**Anticipated Development(s):** Confirmation of a move to a new all-seater stadium has been given. It is planned to be completed in time for the 1997/98 season.

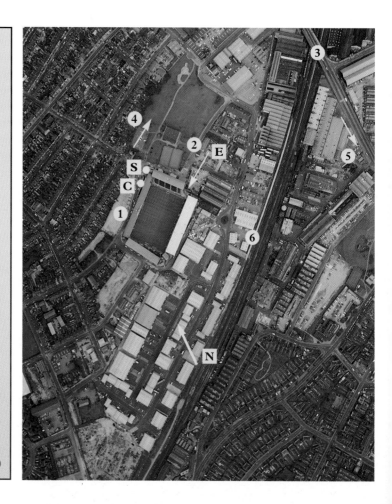

*KEY*
**C** Club Offices
**S** Club Shop
**E** Entrance(s) for visiting supporters

⬆ North direction (approx)

❶ Shaftesbury Crescent
❷ Colombo Street
❸ A514 Osmaston Road
❹ To Derby Midland BR Station (1 mile)
❺ To Ring Road, A6 & M1 Junction 24
❻ Ramsline Halt (BR Specials)

*Left:*
One of a number of Croat internationals recruited by Derby County, Igor Stimac was an impressive player both for Derby during the club's successful season and for Croatia during Euro '96. It will be interesting to see how Derby perform in the Premiership; over the past few seasons the gulf in standards between the top flight and the 1st Division has led to relegation after only one season.

# DONCASTER ROVERS

## Belle Vue, Bawtry Road, Doncaster DN4 5HT

**Tel No:** 01302 539441
**Advance Tickets Tel No:** 01302 539441
**League:** 3rd Division
**Brief History:** Founded 1879. Former Grounds: Town Moor, Belle Vue (not current Ground), Deaf School Playing Field (later name Intake Ground), Bennetthorpe, moved to Belle Vue (former name Low Pasture) in 1922. Record attendance 37,099.
**(Total) Current Capacity:** 8,608 (1,259 seated)
**Visiting Supporters' Allocation:** 1,608
**Club Colours:** Red Shirts and Shorts.

**Nearest Railway Station:** Doncaster
**Parking (Car):** Car Park at ground
**Parking (Coach/Bus):** Car Park at ground
**Police Force and Tel No:** South Yorkshire (01302 366744)
**Disabled Visitors' Facilities**
  **Wheelchairs:** Bawtry Road
  **Blind:** No special facility
**Anticipated Development(s):** The club hopes to relocate to a new site but nothing has been confirmed.

### KEY

**C** Club Offices
**S** Club Shop
**E** Entrance(s) for visiting supporters
**R** Refreshment bars for visiting supporters
**T** Toilets for visiting supporters

⬆ North direction (approx)

❶ A638 Bawtry Road
❷ Racecourse
❸ Car Park
❹ To Doncaster BR Station & A1(M) (3 miles)
❺ To A630 & M18 Junction 4

*Left:*
**Spot the ball! Rover's Graham Jones demonstrates almost balletic grace as he chips the ball in this August 1995 encounter.**

# EVERTON

## Goodison Park, Goodison Road, Liverpool, L4 4EL

**Tel No:** 0151 330 2200
**Advance Tickets Tel No:** 0151 330 2300
**Dial a Seat:** 0151 525 1231
**League:** FA Premier
**Brief History:** Founded 1879 as St. Domingo, changed to Everton in 1880. Former Grounds: Stanley Park, Priory Road and Anfield (Liverpool F.C. Ground), moved to Goodison Park in 1892. Founder-members Football League (1888). Record attendance 78,229.
**(Total) Current Capacity:** 40,200 all seated

**Visiting Supporters' Allocation:** 3,000
**Club Colours:** Blue shirts, white shorts
**Nearest Railway Station:** Liverpool Lime Street
**Parking (Car):** Corner of Utting & Priory Avenues
**Parking (Coach/Bus):** Priory Road
**Police Force and Tel No:** Merseyside (0151 709 6010)
**Disabled Visitors' Facilities**
  **Wheelchairs:** Park End Stand.
  **Blind:** Commentary available

### KEY

- **C** Club Offices
- **S** Club Shop
- **E** Entrance(s) for visiting supporters
- **R** Refreshment bars for visiting supporters
- **T** Toilets for visiting supporters

↑ North direction (approx)

- ❶ A580 Walton Road
- ❷ Bullens Road
- ❸ Goodison Road
- ❹ Car Park
- ❺ Liverpool Lime Street BR Station (2 miles)
- ❻ To M57 Junction 2, 4 and 5
- ❼ Stanley Park

*Right:*
**Following his controversial
(and long delayed) move
from Old Trafford Andrei
Kanchelskis has
established himself as a
firm favourite at Goodison.**

# EXETER CITY

## St. James Park, Exeter, EX4 6PX

**Tel No:** 01392 54073
**Advance Tickets Tel No:** 01392 54073
**League:** 3rd Division
**Brief History:** Founded in 1904. (From amalgamation of St. Sidwell United and Exeter United.) Founder-members Third Division (1920). Record attendance 20,984.
**(Total) Current Capacity:** 10,570 (1,690 seated)
**Visiting Supporters' Allocation:** 1,274
**Club Colours:** Red and white striped shirts, white shorts
**Nearest Railway Station:** Exeter St. James Park
**Parking (Car):** National Car Park and Council Car Parks (No street parking)
**Parking (Coach/Bus):** Paris Street bus station
**Police Force and Tel No:** Devon and Cornwall (01392 52101)
**Disabled Visitors' Facilities**
**Wheelchairs:** St. James Road entrance (prior booking)
**Blind:** No special facility
**Anticipated Development(s):** Following uncertainty, the city council has bought the ground from Beazer Homes and leased to back to the club. Further developments are unconfirmed.

### KEY

**C** Club Offices
**S** Club Shop
**E** Entrance(s) for visiting supporters
**T** Toilets for visiting supporters

↑ North direction (approx)

❶ Exeter St. James Park BR Station
❷ St. James Road
❸ Old Tiverton Road
❹ Blackboy Road

*Right:*
Whilst City may not have achieved a great deal on the field during the 1995/96 season, at least Exeter was still able to support a league team. Financial problems had almost brought the club's demise and the end of the 1995/96 season brought fresh uncertainty over the position of the ground. News that the city council has bought the freehold of St James should ensure that the club retains a home base. Experienced Mark Chamberlain is seen in action with the Grecians on 23 August 1995.

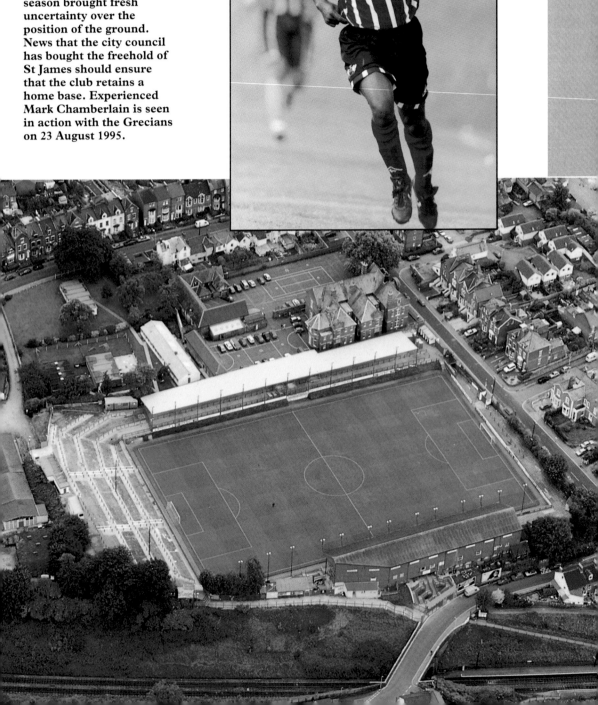

# FULHAM

## Craven Cottage, Stevenage Road, Fulham, London, SW6 6HH

**Tel No:** 0171 736 6561

**Advance Tickets Tel No:** 0171 736 6561

**League:** 3rd Division

**Brief History:** Founded in 1879 as St. Andrews Fulham, changed name to Fulham in 1898. Former Grounds: Star Road, Ranelagh Club, Lillie Road, Eel Brook Common, Purser's Cross, Barn Elms and Half Moon (Wasps Rugby Football Ground), moved to Craven Cottage in 1894. Record attendance 49,335.

**(Total) Current Capacity:** 14,969 (5,119 seated)

**Visiting Supporters' Allocation:** approx 2,800

**Club Colours:** White shirts, black shorts

**Nearest Railway Station:** Putney Bridge (Tube)

**Parking (Car):** Street parking

**Parking (Coach/Bus):** Stevenage Road

**Police Force and Tel No:** Metropolitan (0171 741 6212)

**Disabled Visitors' Facilities**

　**Wheelchairs:** Main Stand

　**Blind:** No special facility

---

*KEY*

**C** Club Offices (The Cottage)

**S** Club Shop

**E** Entrance(s) for visiting supporters

**R** Refreshment bars for visiting supporters

**T** Toilets for visiting supporters

↑ North direction (approx)

**❶** River Thames

**❷** Stevenage Road

**❸** Finlay Street

**❹** Putney Bridge Tube Station (½ mile)

*Left:*
**Fulham is the only league team sponsored by a trade union and perhaps that was why it made hard work of the 1995/96 season despite (or because of?) the knowledge of chairman Jimmy Hill. Micky Adams proudly displays his GMB shirt.**

# GILLINGHAM

## Priestfield Stadium, Redfern Avenue, Gillingham, Kent, ME7 4DD

**Tel No:** 01634 851854
**Advance Tickets Tel No:** 01634 576828
**League:** 2nd Division
**Brief History:** Founded 1893, as New Brompton, changed name to Gillingham in 1913. Founder-members Third Division (1920). Lost Football League status (1938), re-elected to Third Division South (1950). Record attendance 23,002.
**(Total) Current Capacity:** 10,422 (1,225 seated)
**Visiting Supporters' Allocation:** 1,900

**Club Colours:** Blue shirts, blue shorts
**Nearest Railway Station:** Gillingham
**Parking (Car):** Street parking
**Parking (Coach/Bus):** As directed by Police
**Police Force and Tel No:** Kent (01634 834488)
**Disabled Visitors' Facilities**
  **Wheelchairs:** Redfern Avenue
  **Blind:** No special facility
**Anticipated Development(s):** The club is investigating the possibility of relocation, but nothing is confirmed.

### KEY

**C** Club Offices
**S** Club Shop
**E** Entrance(s) for visiting supporters
**R** Refreshment bars for visiting supporters
**T** Toilets for visiting supporters

↑ North direction (approx)

❶ Redfern Avenue
❷ Toronto Road
❸ Gordon Road
❹ Gillingham BR Station (¼ mile)
❺ Woodlands Road

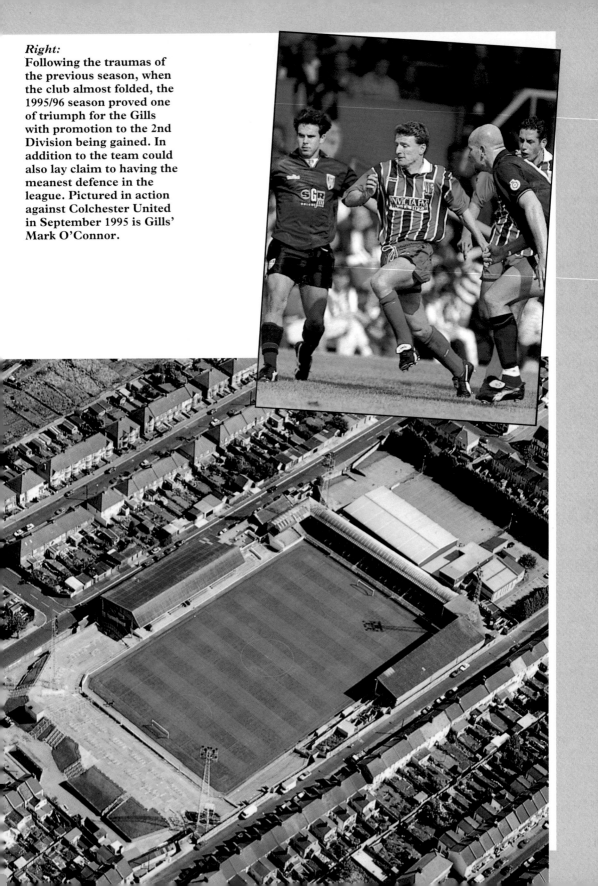

*Right:*

Following the traumas of the previous season, when the club almost folded, the 1995/96 season proved one of triumph for the Gills with promotion to the 2nd Division being gained. In addition to the team could also lay claim to having the meanest defence in the league. Pictured in action against Colchester United in September 1995 is Gills' Mark O'Connor.

# GRIMSBY TOWN

## Blundell Park, Cleethorpes, DN35 7PY

**Tel No:** 01472 697111
**Advance Tickets Tel No:** 01472 697111
**League:** 1st Division
**Brief History:** Founded 1878, as Grimsby Pelham, changed name to Grimsby Town in 1879. Former Grounds: Clee Park (two adjacent fields) & Abbey Park, moved to Blundell Park in 1899. Founder-members 2nd Division (1892). Record attendance 31,651.
**(Total) Current Capacity:** 8,686 (all seated)
**Visiting Supporters' Allocation:** 1,874

**Club Colours:** Black & white striped shirts, black shorts
**Nearest Railway Station:** Cleethorpes
**Parking (Car):** Street Parking
**Parking (Coach/Bus):** Harrington Street
**Police Force and Tel No:** Humberside (01472 359171)
**Disabled Visitors' Facilities**
  **Wheelchairs:** Harrington Street
  **Blind:** Commentary available

**KEY**
- **C** Club Offices (Findus Stand)
- **S** Club Shop
- **E** Entrance(s) for visiting supporters
- **R** Refreshment bars for visiting supporters
- **T** Toilets for visiting supporters

⬆ North direction (approx)

❶ A180 Grimsby Road
❷ Cleethorpes BR Station (1½ miles)
❸ To Grimsby and M180 Junction 5
❹ Harrington Street
❺ Constitutional Avenue
❻ Humber Estuary

*Left:*
**A strange season for Grimsby Town; initially the team seems to be on the edges of the promotion race and there is the arrival of the Italian player Bonetti with all the consequent publicity. Then there is the changing room argument between Bonetti and manager Brian Laws and the season ends with the team gradually drifting towards the lower half of the table. Gary Croft looks as though he can't quite believe it all.**

# HARTLEPOOL UNITED

## Victoria Ground, Clarence Road, Hartlepool, TS24 8BZ

**Tel No:** 01429 272584
**Advance Tickets Tel No:** 01429 272584
**League:** 3rd Division
**Brief History:** Founded 1908 as Hartlepools United, changed to Hartlepool (1968) and to Hartlepool United in 1977. Founder-members 3rd Division (1921). Record attendance 17,426.
**(Total) Current Capacity:** 7,229 (3,966 seated)
**Visiting Supporters' Allocation:** 717 (located in Rink Stand)

**Club Colours:** Blue & white striped shirts, Blue shorts
**Nearest Railway Station:** Hartlepool Church Street
**Parking (car):** Street parking and rear of clock garage
**Police Force and Tel No:** Cleveland (01429 221151)
**Disabled Visitors' Facilities**
   **Wheelchairs:** Raby Road
   **Blind:** Commentary available

*KEY*
**C** Club Offices
**S** Club Shop
**E** Entrance(s) for visiting supporters

↑ North direction (approx)

❶ A1088 Clarence Road
❷ Hartlepool Church Street BR Station
❸ A179 Raby Road
❹ Greyhound Stadium
❺ To Middlesbrough A689 & A1(M)

*Right:*
**Veteran striker Joe Allon leads United's attack against promotion chasing Hereford United at Edgar Street on 30 April 1996. Presumably the legend on shirt refers to the sponsor and not to the club's tactics (at least it would make a variation on the long-ball game).**

# HEREFORD UNITED

## Edgar Street, Hereford, HR4 9JU

**Tel No:** 01432 276666
**Advance Tickets Tel No:** 01432 276666
**League:** 3rd Division
**Brief History:** Founded 1924, elected to Football League 1972. Record attendance 18,114
**(Total) Current Capacity:** 9,020 (2,897 seated)
**Visiting Supporters' Allocation:** 1,977
**Club Colours:** White shirts with black trim, black shorts

**Nearest Railway Station:** Hereford
**Parking (Car):** Merton Meadow & Edgar Street
**Parking (Coach/Bus):** Cattle Market
**Police Force and Tel No:** Hereford (01432 276422)
**Disabled Visitors' Facilities**
  **Wheelchairs:** Edgar Street (few)
  **Blind:** Commentary available

---

*KEY*
- **C** Club Offices
- **S** Club Shop
- **E** Entrance(s) for visiting supporters
- **R** Refreshment bars for visiting supporters
- **T** Toilets for visiting supporters

↑ North direction (approx)

❶ A49 Edgar Street
❷ Blackfriars Street
❸ Hereford BR Station (½ mile)
❹ Newmarket Street
❺ To A438 & M50

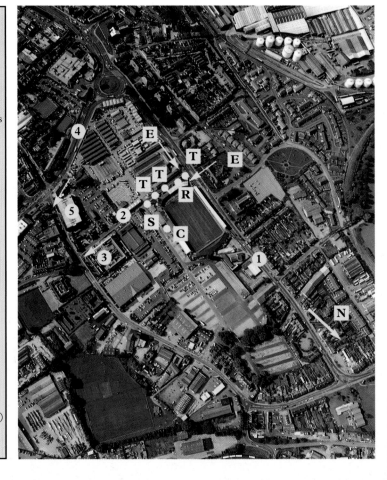

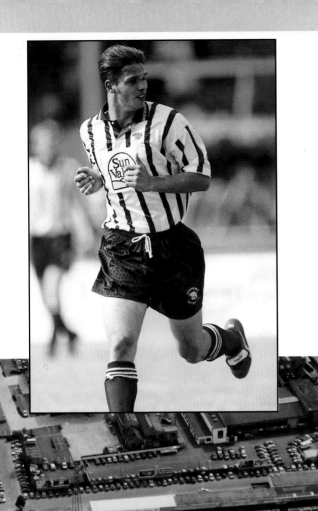

*Left:*
**An improved performance in the league, saw Hereford United in the Play-Off positions come May. Unfortunately, defeat in the first round against Darlington, consigned United to another season in the 3rd Division. Phil Preedy catches the Sun (Valley) in this August 1995 pre-season match.**

# HUDDERSFIELD TOWN

## The Alfred McAlpine Stadium, Leeds Road, Huddersfield, HD1 6PX

**Tel No:** 01484 420335
**Advance Tickets Tel No:** 01484 420335
**League:** 1st Division
**Brief History:** Founded 1908, elected to Football League in 1910. First Club to win the Football League Championship three years in succession. Moved from Leeds Road ground to Kirklees (Alfred McAlpine) Stadium 1994/95 season. Record attendance (Leeds Road) 67,037.
**(Total) Current Capacity:** 19,600 (all seated)
**Visiting Supporters' Allocation:** 4,053 (all seated)
**Club Colours:** Blue and white striped shirts, white shorts

**Nearest Railway Station:** Huddersfield
**Parking (Car):** Car parks adjacent to ground
**Parking (Coach/Bus):** Car parks adjacent to ground
**Police Force and Tel No:** West Yorkshire (01484 422122)
**Disabled Visitors' Facilities**
**Wheelchairs:** Three sides of Ground, at low levels and raised areas, including toilets access.
**Blind:** Area for Partially sighted with Hospital Radio commentary.
**Anticipated Development(s):** It is planned to have the North Stand completed for the start of the 1997/98 season.

---

### KEY
**C** Club Offices
**S** Club Shop
**E** Entrance(s) for visiting supporters
**R** Refreshment bars for visiting supporters
**T** Toilets for visiting supporters

↑ North direction (approx)

❶ To Leeds and M62 Junction 25
❷ A62 Leeds Road
❸ To Huddersfield BR station (1¼ miles)
❹ Disabled parking
❺ Town Avenue pay car park (on site of former ground)
❻ Bradley Mills (permit only car park)
❼ St Andrews pay car park
❽ Coach park

*Right:*
Despite the pundits who thought that Huddersfield, having only gained promotion through winning the Play-Off final at the end of the 1994/95 season, would struggle, Darren Bullock and the rest of the team performed creditably and only just failed to make a Play-Off place for the second season running.

# HULL CITY

## Boothferry Park, Boothferry Road, Hull, HU4 6EU

**Tel No:** 01482 351119
**Advance Tickets Tel No:** 01482 351119
**League:** 3rd Division
**Brief History:** Founded 1904. Former grounds: The Boulevard (Hull Rugby League Ground), Dairycoates, Anlaby Road Cricket Circle (Hull Cricket Ground), Anlaby Road, moved to Boothferry Park in 1946. Record attendance 55,019.
**(Total) Current Capacity:** 12,996 (5,495 seated)
**Visiting Supporters' Allocation:** 2,090 (530 seated)

**Club Colours:** Amber shirts, black shorts
**Nearest Railway Station:** Hull Paragon
**Parking (Car):** Street Parking and at ground (limited)
**Parking (Coach/Bus):** At ground
**Police Force and Tel No:** Humberside (01482 220148)
**Disabled Visitors' Facilities**
   **Wheelchairs:** Corner East/South stands
   **Blind:** Commentary available

---

**KEY**

**C** Club Offices
**E** Entrance(s) for visiting supporters

↑ North direction (approx)

❶ A63 Boothferry Road
❷ North Road
❸ Hull Paragon BR Station (1½ miles)
❹ To Humber Bridge and M62 Junction 38

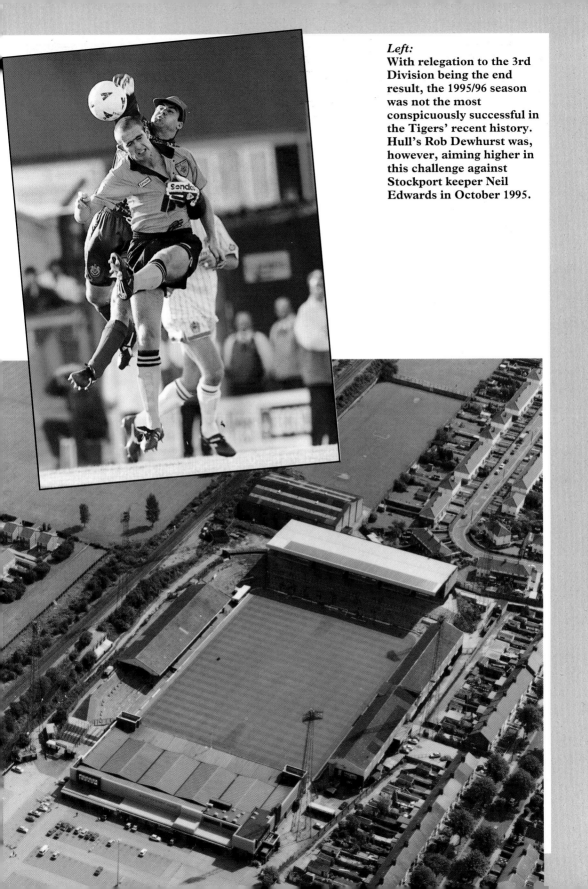

*Left:*
With relegation to the 3rd Division being the end result, the 1995/96 season was not the most conspicuously successful in the Tigers' recent history. Hull's Rob Dewhurst was, however, aiming higher in this challenge against Stockport keeper Neil Edwards in October 1995.

# IPSWICH TOWN

## Portman Road, Ipswich, IP1 2DA

**Tel No:** 01473 219211

**Advance Tickets Tel No:** 01473 221133

**League:** 1st Division

**Brief History:** Founded 1887 as Ipswich Association F.C., changed to Ipswich Town in 1888. Former Grounds: Broom Hill & Brookes Hall, moved to Portman Road in 1888. Record attendance 38,010

**(Total) Current Capacity:** 22,500 all seated

**Visiting Supporters Allocation:** 2,200 seated

**Club Colours:** Blue shirts, white shorts

**Nearest Railway Station:** Ipswich

**Parking (Car):** Portman Road, Portman Walk & West End Road

**Parking (Coach/Bus):** West End Road

**Police Force and Tel No:** Suffolk (01473 611611)

**Disabled Visitors' Facilities**
  **Wheelchairs:** Lower Pioneer Stand
  **Blind:** Commentary available

---

**KEY**

**C** Club Offices

**S** Club Shop

**E** Entrance(s) for visiting supporters

**R** Refreshment bars for visiting supporters

**T** Toilets for visiting supporters

⬆ North direction (approx)

❶ A137 West End Road
❷ Portman Walk
❸ Portman Road
❹ Princes Street
❺ Ipswich BR Station
❻ Car Parks

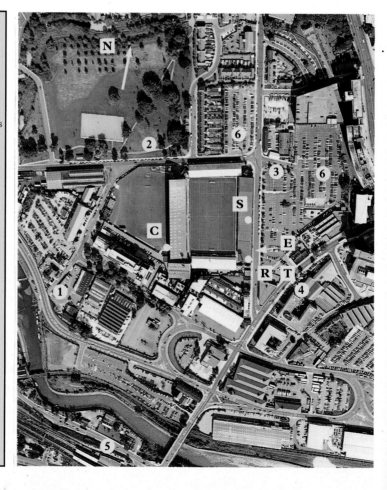

*Left:*
Although missing out at the end, Ipswich always seemed to be threatening for a Play-Off place following the club's relegation from the Premiership at the end of the 1994/95 season. Experienced keeper Craig Forrest remains an important part of the Town set-up as the club looks forward to mounting another challenge in the 1st Division.

# LEEDS UNITED

## Elland Road, Leeds, LS11 0ES

**Tel No:** 0113 271 6037
**Advance Tickets Tel No:** 0113 271 0710
**League:** F.A. Premier
**Brief History:** Founded 1919, formed from the former 'Leeds City' Club, who were disbanded following expulsion from the Football League in October 1919. Joined Football League in 1920. Record attendance 57,892
**(Total) Current Capacity:** 40,000 (all seated)
**Visiting Supporters' Allocation:** 2,200 seated

**Club Colours:** White shirts, white shorts
**Nearest Railway Station:** Leeds City
**Parking (Car):** Car parks adjacent to ground
**Parking (Coach/Bus):** As directed by Police
**Police Force and Tel No:** West Yorkshire (0113 243 5353)
**Disabled Visitors' Facilities**
　**Wheelchairs:** West Stand and South Stand
　**Blind:** Commentary available

*KEY*
**C**　Club Offices
**S**　Club Shop
**E**　Entrance(s) for visiting supporters

↑　North direction (approx)

❶　M621
❷　M621 Junction 2
❸　A643 Elland Road
❹　Lowfields Road
❺　To A58

*Right:*
Few at Elland Road would claim that the 1995/96 season was amongst United's greatest. Although the club reached the final of the Coca Cola Cup, the abject performance was perhaps symptomatic of the team's failure to achieve more than mid-table mediocrity. One of Howard Wilkinson's high profile acquisitions was the Swede Tomas Brolin, who never really fulfilled the high expectations following his multi-million pound transfer.

# LEICESTER CITY

## City Stadium, Filbert Street, Leicester, LE2 7FL

**Tel No:** 0116 255 5000

**Advance Tickets Tel No:** 0116 255 5000

**League:** F.A. Premier

**Brief History:** Founded 1884 as Leicester Fosse, changed name to Leicester City in 1919. Former Grounds: Fosse Road South, Victoria Road, Belgrave Cycle Track, Mill Lane & Aylestone Road Cricket Ground, moved to Filbert Street in 1891. Record attendance 47,298

**(Total) Current Capacity:** 22,500 (all seated)

**Visiting Supporters' Allocation:** approx 1,800

**Club Colours:** Blue shirts, white shorts

**Nearest Railway Station:** Leicester

**Parking (Car):** NCP car park & street parking

**Parking (Coach/Bus):** Western Boulevard

**Police Force and Tel No:** Leicester (0116 253 0066)

**Disabled Visitors' Facilities**
    **Wheelchairs:** Filbert Street
    **Blind:** No special facility

### KEY

**C** Club Offices

**S** Club Shop

**E** Entrance(s) for visiting supporters

**R** Refreshment bars for visiting supporters

**T** Toilets for visiting supporters

↑ North direction (approx)

**❶** Walnut Street
**❷** Filbert Street
**❸** Grasmere Street
**❹** River Soar
**❺** M1 and M69 Junction 21
**❻** Leicester BR Station (1 mile)

*Right:*
One of a number of teams apparently destined to lead a yo-yo existence between the FA Carling Premiership and the 1st Division — lacking the resources to stay up once promoted but too strong for the lower division — Leicester City bounced straight back to the Premiership through victory over Crystal Palace in the 1st Division Play-Off Final. The Foxes' Steve Walsh is featured here.

# LEYTON ORIENT

## Leyton Stadium, Brisbane Road, Leyton, London, E10 5NE

**Tel No:** 0181 539 2223
**Advance Tickets Tel No:** 0181 539 2223
**League:** 3rd Division
**Brief History:** Founded 1887 as Clapton Orient, from Eagle Cricket Club (formerly Glyn Cricket Club formed in 1881). Changed name to Leyton Orient (1946), Orient (1966), Leyton Orient (1987). Former grounds: Glyn Road, Whittles Athletic Ground, Millfields Road, Lea Bridge Road, Wembley Stadium (2 games), moved to Brisbane Road in 1937. Record attendance 34,345.
**(Total) Current Capacity:** 17,065 (7,133 seated)
**Visiting Supporters' Allocation:** 4,179

**Club Colours:** Red shirts, black shorts
**Nearest Railway Station:** Leyton (tube), Leyton Midland Road
**Parking (Car):** Street parking
**Parking (Coach/Bus):** As directed by Police
**Police Force and Tel No:** Metropolitan (0181 556 8855)
**Disabled Visitors Facilities**
  **Wheelchairs:** Windsor Road
  **Blind:** Match commentary supplied on request
**Anticipated Development(s):** Work will start on the redevelopment of the South Terrace as a new 2,900-seat stand during the 1996/97 season. This will reduce the ground's capacity to approximately 14,000 during construction.

### KEY

**C** Club Offices
**S** Club Shop
**E** Entrance(s) for visiting supporters
**R** Refreshment bars for visiting supporters
**T** Toilets for visiting supporters

↑ North direction (approx)

❶ Buckingham Road
❷ Oliver Road
❸ A112 High Road Leyton
❹ Leyton Tube Station (¼ mile)
❺ Brisbane Road

*Left:*
**Much was expected of Leyton Orient following their relegation to the 3rd Division, but like another London club (Fulham) which once aspired to be amongst football's elite, the club struggled to achieve anything more than a mid-table position. Joe Baker demonstrates his skill in the game against Cambridge United on 4 May 1996.**

# LINCOLN CITY

## Sincil Bank, Lincoln, LN5 8LD

**Tel No:** 01522 522224
**Advance Tickets Tel No:** 01522 522224
**League:** 3rd Division
**Brief History:** Founded 1884. Former Ground: John O'Gaunts Ground, moved to Sincil Bank in 1895. Founder-members 2nd Division Football League (1892). Relegated from 4th Division in 1987, promoted from GM Vauxhall Conference in 1988. Record attendance 23,196.
**(Total) Current Capacity:** 10,918 (9,246 seated)

**Visiting Supporters' Allocation:** 2,425 (all seated)
**Club Colours:** Red & white striped shirts, black shorts
**Nearest Railway Station:** Lincoln Central
**Parking (Car):** Adjacent Ground
**Parking (Coach/Bus):** South Common
**Police Force and Tel No:** Lincolnshire (01522 529911)
**Disabled Visitors' Facilities**
  **Wheelchairs:** South Park Stand
  **Blind:** No special facility

---

### KEY

**C** Club Offices
**S** Club Shop
**E** Entrance(s) for visiting supporters
**R** Refreshment bars for visiting supporters
**T** Toilets for visiting supporters

↑ North direction (approx)

❶ A46 High Street
❷ Sincil Bank
❸ Sausthorpe Street
❹ Cross Street
❺ A158 Canwick Road
❻ A158 South Park Avenue
❼ Car Park
❽ Lincoln Central BR Station (1/2 mile)

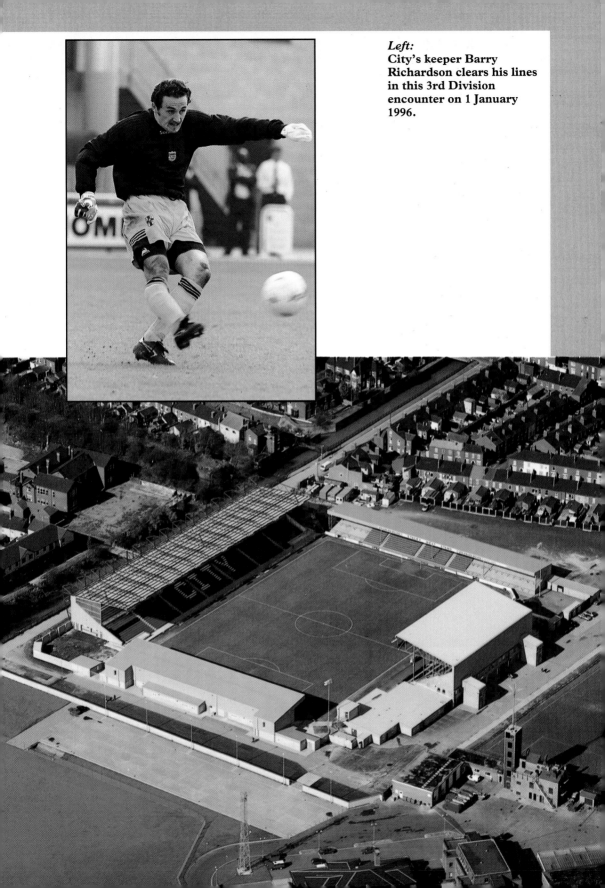

*Left:*
**City's keeper Barry Richardson clears his lines in this 3rd Division encounter on 1 January 1996.**

# LIVERPOOL

## Anfield Road, Liverpool, L4 0TH

**Tel No:** 0151 263 2361
**Advance Tickets Tel No:** 0151 260 8680
**League:** F.A. Premier
**Brief History:** Founded 1892. Anfield Ground formerly Everton F.C. Ground. Joined Football League in 1893. Record attendance 61,905.
**(Total) Current Capacity:** Approx 41,000 (all seated)
**Visiting Supporters' Allocation:** 1,600
**Club Colours:** Red shirts, red shorts

**Nearest Railway Station:** Kirkdale
**Parking (Car):** Stanley car park
**Parking (Coach/Bus):** Priory Road & Pinehurst Avenue
**Police Force and Tel No:** Merseyside (0151 709 6010)
**Disabled Visitors' Facilities**
   **Wheelchairs:** Kop and Main Stands
   **Blind:** Commentary available

*KEY*

**C** Club Offices
**S** Club Shop
**E** Entrance(s) for visiting supporters

↑ North direction (approx)

❶ Car Park
❷ Anfield Road
❸ A5089 Walton Breck Road
❹ Kemlyn Road
❺ Kirkdale BR Station (1 mile)
❻ Utting Avenue
❼ Stanley Park
❽ Spion Kop

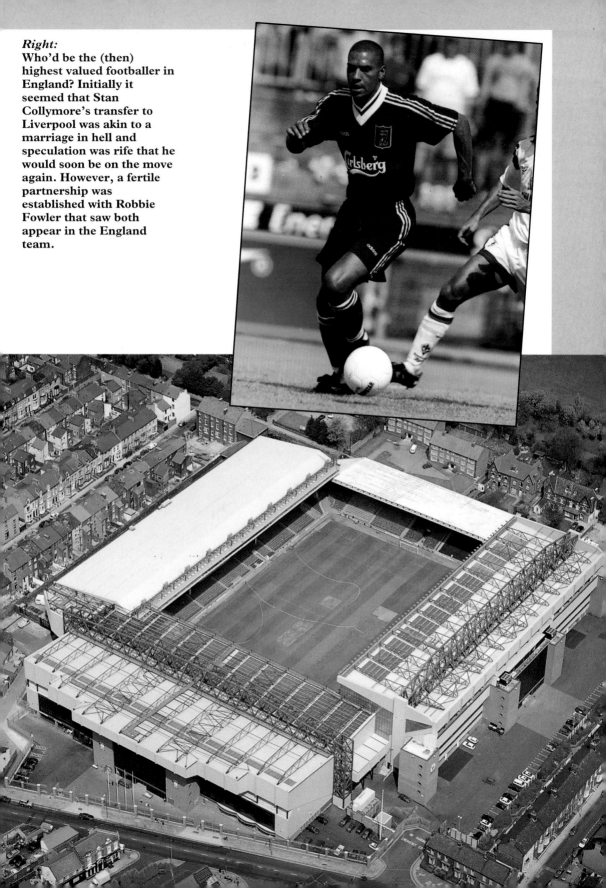

*Right:*
Who'd be the (then) highest valued footballer in England? Initially it seemed that Stan Collymore's transfer to Liverpool was akin to a marriage in hell and speculation was rife that he would soon be on the move again. However, a fertile partnership was established with Robbie Fowler that saw both appear in the England team.

# LUTON TOWN

## Kenilworth Road Stadium, 1 Maple Road, Luton, LU4 8AW

**Tel No:** 01582 411622
**Advance Tickets Tel No:** 01582 416976
**League:** 2nd Division
**Brief History:** Founded 1885 from an amalgamation of Wanderers F.C. & Excelsior F.C. Former Grounds: Dallow Lane & Dunstable Road, moved to Kenilworth Road in 1905. Record attendance 30,069.
**(Total) Current Capacity:** 9,975 (all seated)
**Visiting Supporters' Allocation:** 2,257
**Club Colours:** White shirts with royal blue & orange stripe on collar & waist. Royal blue shorts with white & orange trim.

**Nearest Railway Station:** Luton
**Parking (Car):** Street parking
**Parking (Coach/Bus):** Luton bus station
**Police Force and Tel No:** Bedfordshire (01582 401212)
**Disabled Visitors' Facilities**
  **Wheelchairs:** Kenilworth Road
  **Blind:** Commentary available
**Anticipated Development(s):** With the lease on Kenilworth Road soon to expire, the club is investigating a number of options for its future location.

### KEY
**C** Club Offices
**S** Club Shop
**E** Entrance(s) for visiting supporters
**R** Refreshment bars for visiting supporters
**T** Toilets for visiting supporters

↑ North direction (approx)

❶ To M1 Junction 11
❷ Wimborne Road
❸ Kenilworth Road
❹ Oak Road
❺ Dunstable Road
❻ Luton BR Station (1 mile)
❼ Ticket Office

*Left:*
**Despite the presence of ex-Ipswich Town Bulgarian striker Bontcho Guentchev and the managership of Lennie Lawrence — who claimed to enjoy the struggle of lifting teams out of the relegation zone — the Hatters finished a disastrous 1995/96 season by being relegated to the 2nd Division.**

# MANCHESTER CITY

## Maine Road, Moss Side, Manchester, M14 7WN

**Tel No:** 0161 224 5000
**Advance Tickets Tel No:** 0161 226 2224
**League:** 1st Division
**Brief History:** Founded 1880 as West Gorton, changed name to Ardwick (reformed 1887) and to Manchester City in 1894. Former grounds: Clowes Street, Kirkmanshulme Cricket Club, Donkey Common, Pink Bank Lane & Hyde Road, moved to Maine Road in 1923. Founder-members 2nd Division (1892). Record attendance 84,569 (record for Football League ground).
**(Total) Current Capacity:** 32,500 (all seated)
**Visiting Supporters' Allocation:** 2,248

**Club Colours:** Sky blue shirts, white shorts
**Nearest Railway Station:** Manchester Piccadilly (2½ miles)
**Parking (Car):** Street parking & local schools
**Parking (Coach/Bus):** Kippax Street car park
**Police Force and Tel No:** Greater Manchester (0161 872 5050)
**Disabled Visitors' Facilities**
  **Wheelchairs:** Umbro Stand / Kippax Stand
  **Blind:** Main Stand 'G' Block
**Anticipated Developments(s):** The next phase will be the construction of a corner stand linking the Kippax and North stands. The actual date of construction is unconfirmed.

### KEY

**C** Club Offices
**S** Club Shop
**E** Entrance(s) for visiting supporters

↑ North direction (approx)

❶ Thornton Road
❷ South Upper Lloyd Street
❸ To A5103 Princess Road
❹ To City Centre and Manchester Piccadilly BR Station (2½ miles)
❺ To A6010 & M31 Junction 7
❻ Maine Road

*Left:*
**There was great optimism
at Maine Road following
the take-over by Francis
Lee and the appointment
of Alan Ball as manager.
As so often, however, the
pre-season dreams turned
into a nightmare as City
started off disastrously and
despite a number of good
performances were unable
to stave off relegation.
Demotion came despite the
scoring skills of Uwe
Rosler and the silky skills
of the other overseas
imports in the City team.**

# MANCHESTER UNITED

## Old Trafford, Warwick Road North, Manchester, M16 0RA

**Tel No:** 0161 872 1661
**Advance Tickets Tel No:** 0161 872 0199
**League:** F.A. Premier
**Brief History:** Founded in 1878 as 'Newton Heath L & Y', later Newton Heath, changed to Manchester United in 1902. Former Grounds: North Road, Monsall & Bank Street, Clayton, moved to Old Trafford in 1910 (used Manchester City F.C. Ground 1941-49). Founder-members Second Division (1892). Record attendance 76,962.
**(Total) Current Capacity:** 55,300 (all seated).
**Visiting Supporters' Allocation:** Approx. 3,000

**Club Colours:** Red shirts, white shorts
**Nearest Railway Station:** At Ground
**Parking (Car):** Lancashire Cricket Ground & White City
**Parking (Coach/Bus):** As directed by Police
**Police Force and Tel No:** Greater Manchester (0161 872 5050)
**Disabled Visitors' Facilities**
  **Wheelchairs:** South East Stand.
  **Blind:** Commentary available
**Anticipated Development(s):** With the completion of the North Stand nothing definite is planned.

---

*KEY*
**C** Club Offices
**S** Club Shop

↑ North direction (approx)

❶ A5081 Trafford Park Road to M63 Junction 4 (5 miles)
❷ A56 Chester Road
❸ Manchester Ship Canal
❹ Old Trafford Cricket Ground
❺ To Parking and Warwick Road BR Station

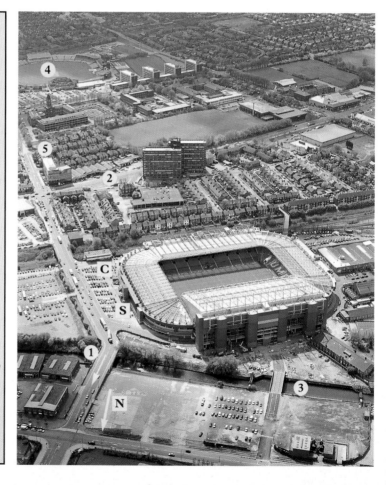

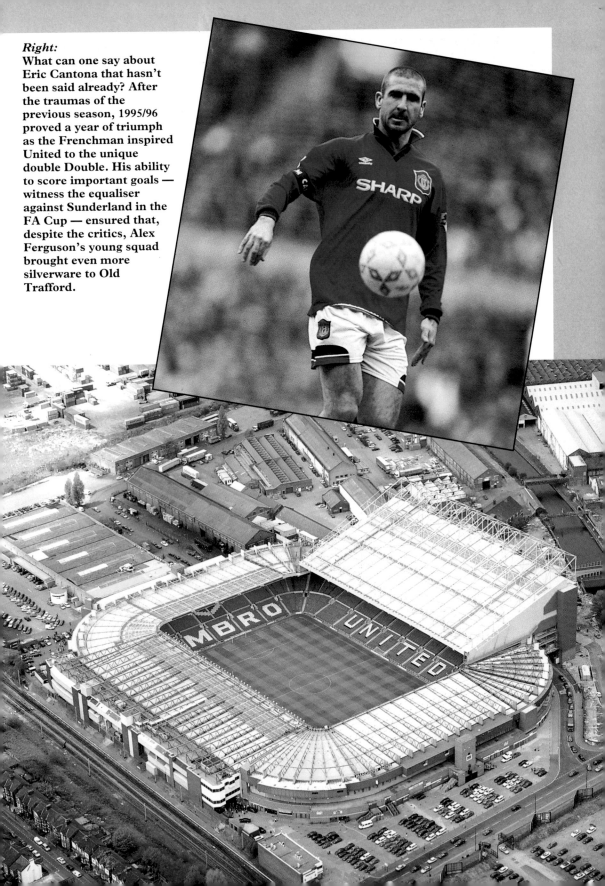

**Right:**
What can one say about Eric Cantona that hasn't been said already? After the traumas of the previous season, 1995/96 proved a year of triumph as the Frenchman inspired United to the unique double Double. His ability to score important goals — witness the equaliser against Sunderland in the FA Cup — ensured that, despite the critics, Alex Ferguson's young squad brought even more silverware to Old Trafford.

# MANSFIELD TOWN

## Field Mill Ground, Quarry Lane, Mansfield, Notts

**Tel No:** 01623 23567
**Advance Tickets Tel No:** 01623 23567
**League:** 3rd Division
**Brief History:** Founded 1910 as Mansfield
Wesleyans Boys Brigade, changed to Mansfield
Town in 1914. Former Grounds: Pelham
Street, Newgate Lane & The Prairie, moved to
Field Mill in 1919. Record attendance 24,467.
**(Total) Current Capacity:** 7,033 (2,863 seated)
**Visiting Supporters' Allocation:** 2,028 (564
seated)
**Club Colours:** Amber with blue trim shirts,
Amber shorts with blue trim.

**Nearest Railway Station:** Mansfield
**Parking (Car):** Car park at Ground
**Parking (Coach/Bus):** Car park at Ground
**Police Force and Tel No:** Nottinghamshire
(01623 420999)
**Disabled Visitors' Facilities**
  **Wheelchairs:** Bishop Street
  (Entrance at North end of West stand)
  **Blind:** Commentary available
**Anticipated Development(s):** The club hopes
to move to a new site for the start of the
1997/98 season.

**KEY**

**C** Club Offices
**E** Entrance(s) for visiting
supporters

↑ North direction (approx)

❶ Car Park
❷ Quarry Lane
❸ A60 Nottingham Road to M1
Junction 27
❹ Portland Street
❺ To A38 and M1 Junction 28
❻ Town Centre

*Left:*
**Town's Steve Parkin suggests where he thinks the ball ought to go in this cup clash with Crewe Alexandra on 2 December 1995 at Gresty Road.**

# MIDDLESBROUGH

## The Cellnet Riverside Stadium, Middlesbrough, Cleveland

**Tel No:** 01642 227227
**League:** FA Premier
**Brief History:** Founded 1876. Former Grounds: Archery Ground (Albert Park), Breckon Hill Road, Linthorpe Road, moved to Ayresome Park in 1903, and to current ground in Summer 1995. FA Amateur Cup winners 1894 and 1897 (joined Football League in 1899). Record attendance (Ayresome Park) 53,596.
**(Total) Current Capacity:** Approx. 30,000 (all seated)
**Visiting Supporters' Allocation:** 2,470 (in the South Stand)
**Club Colours:** Red shirts with white yoke, white shorts

**Nearest Railway Station:** Middlesbrough
**Parking (Car):** All parking at stadium is for permit holders.
**Parking (Coach/Bus):** As directed
**Police Force and Tel No:** Cleveland (01642 248184)
**Disabled Visitors' Facilities**
  **Wheelchairs:** More than 300 places available for disabled fans.
  **Blind:** Commentary available.
**Anticipated Development(s):** Plans are in hand for the construction of the missing two corner stands to increase capacity to c35,000.

### KEY
**C** Club Offices
**S** Club Shop

↑ North direction (approx)

❶ Cargo Fleet Road
❷ To Middlesbrough station (0.5 miles)
❸ Middlesbrough town centre
❹ Middlesbrough Docks (1 mile) and Town Centre
❺ A66
❻ Station Street (leading to Borough Road)
❼ Car Park
❽ South Stand

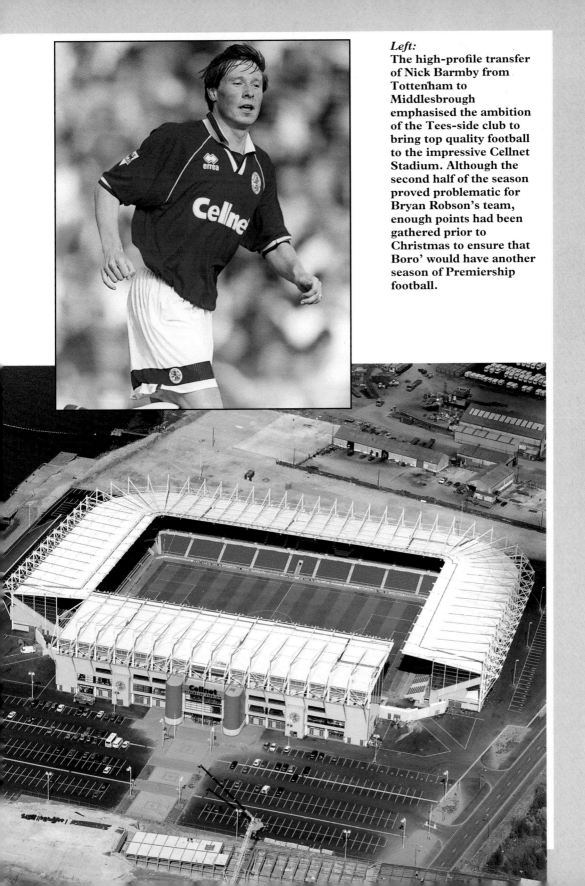

*Left:*
**The high-profile transfer of Nick Barmby from Tottenham to Middlesbrough emphasised the ambition of the Tees-side club to bring top quality football to the impressive Cellnet Stadium. Although the second half of the season proved problematic for Bryan Robson's team, enough points had been gathered prior to Christmas to ensure that Boro' would have another season of Premiership football.**

# MILLWALL

## New Den, Bolina Road, London, SE16

**Tel No:** 0171 232 1222
**Advance Tickets Tel No:** 0171 231 9999
**League:** 2nd Division
**Brief History:** Founded 1885 as Millwall
Rovers, changed name to Millwall Athletic
(1889) and Millwall (1925). Former Grounds:
Glengall Road, East Ferry Road (2 separate
Grounds), North Greenwich Ground and The
Den - Cold Blow Lane - moved to New Den
1993/94 season. Founder-members Third
Division (1920). Record attendance (at The
Den) 48,672.
**(Total) Current Capacity:** 20,150 (20,150
seated)

**Visiting Supporters' Allocation:** 4,382
**Club Colours:** Royal Blue shirts, blue shorts
**Nearest Railway Station:** South Bermondsey or
Surrey Docks (tube)
**Parking (Car):** Juno Way car parking (8 mins. walk)
**Parking (Coach/Bus):** At Ground
**Police Force and Tel No:** Metropolitan (0171
679 9217)
**Disabled Visitors' Facilities**
**Wheelchairs:** Area allocated
**Blind:** Commentary available

*KEY*
**C** Club Offices
**S** Club Shop
**E** Entrance(s) for visiting
supporters

↑ North direction (approx)

❶ Bolina Road
❷ South Bermondsey BR
❸ Surrey Quays Underground
❹ Rotherhithe Tunnel
❺ Ilderton Road
❻ The 'Old' Den
❼ River Thames

# NEWCASTLE UNITED

## St. James' Park, Newcastle-upon-Tyne, NE1 4ST

**Tel No:** 0191 201 8400
**Advance Tickets Tel No:** 0191 261 1571
**League:** F. A. Premier
**Brief History:** Founded in 1882 as Newcastle East End, changed to Newcastle United in 1892. Former Grounds: Chillingham Road, moved to St. James' Park (former home of defunct Newcastle West End) in 1892. Record attendance 68,386.
**(Total) Current Capacity:** 37,000 (all seated)
**Visiting Supporters' Allocation:** 1,700

**Club Colours:** Black & white striped shirts, black shorts
**Nearest Railway Station**: Newcastle Central
**Parking (Car):** Leazes car park & street parking
**Parking (Coach/Bus):** Leazes car park
**Police Force and Tel No:** Northumbria (0191 232 3451)
**Disabled Visitors' Facilities**
  **Wheelchairs:** Sir John Hall Stand
  **Blind:** Commentary available

---

*KEY*
**C** Club Offices
**E** Entrance(s) for visiting supporters
**S** Club Shop

↑ North direction (approx)

❶ St. James' Street
❷ Strawberry Place
❸ Gallowgate
❹ Wellington Street
❺ To Newcastle Central BR Station (1/2 mile) & A6127 (M)
❻ Car Park

*Right:*
1995/96 *should* have been the season that United won the Championship for the first time since World War 2 — the team led the table with games in hand for many months. And yet it all went horribly wrong. One school of thought has it that United's loss of form resulted from the inclusion of Columbian Faustino Asprilla in the team, with the consequent change of tactics.

# NORTHAMPTON TOWN

## Sixfields Stadium, Northampton, NN5 5QA

**Tel No:** 01604 757773

**League:** 3rd Division

**Brief History:** Founded 1897. Former, County, Ground was part of Northamptonshire County Cricket Ground. Moved to Sixfields Stadium during early 1994/95 season. Record attendance 24,523 (at County Ground)

**(Total) Current Capacity:** 7,653 (all seated)

**Visiting Supporters' Allocation:** 1,367 (all seated)

**Club Colours:** Claret shirts, White shorts

**Nearest Railway Station:** Northampton Castle

**Parking (Car):** Adjacent to Ground

**Parking (Coach/Bus):** Adjacent to Ground

**Police Force and Tel No:** Northants (01604 33221)

**Disabled Visitors' Facilities**

  **Wheelchairs:** Available on all four sides.

  **Blind:** Available.

---

*KEY*

**C** Club Offices

**S** Club Shop

**E** Entrance(s) for visiting supporters

**R** Refreshment bars for visiting supporters

**T** Toilets for visiting supporters

↑ North direction (approx)

❶ Weedon Road to Town Centre and Northampton Castle BR station (two miles)

❷ Upton Way, to M1 Junction 15A

❸ A45, to M1 Junction 16

❹ Car parks

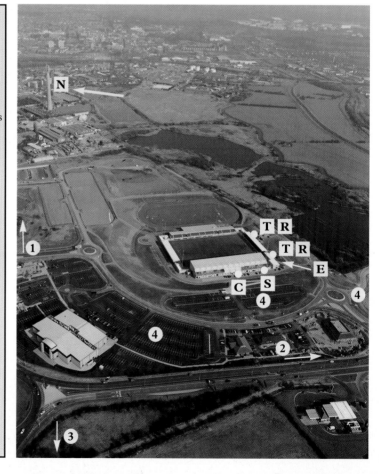

112

*Right:*
**Town's Ray Warburton
appears to be directing the
traffic in this 3rd Division
clash at the Sixfields
Stadium against Fulham
on 30 September 1995.**

# NORWICH CITY

## Carrow Road, Norwich, NR1 1JE

**Tel No:** 01603 760760
**Advance Tickets Tel No:** 01603 761661
**League:** 1st Division
**Brief History:** Founded 1902. Former grounds: Newmarket Road and the Nest, Rosary Road; moved to Carrow Road in 1935. Founder members 3rd Division (1920). Record attendance 43,984.
**(Total) Current Capacity:** 21,972 (seated)
**Visiting Supporters' Allocation:** 1,741

**Club Colours:** Yellow shirts, green shorts
**Nearest Railway Station:** Norwich
**Parking (Car):** City centre car parks
**Parking (Coach/Bus):** Lower Clarence Road
**Police Force and Tel No:** Norfolk (01603 621212)
**Disabled Visitors' Facilities**
  **Wheelchairs:** South Stand (heated)
  **Blind:** No special facility

### KEY
**C** Club Offices
**S** Club Shop
**E** Entrance(s) for visiting supporters

↑ North direction (approx)

❶ Carrow Road
❷ A47 King Street
❸ River Wensum
❹ Riverside
❺ Car Park
❻ Norwich BR Station

*Left:*
After the club's relegation at the end of the 1994/95 season, the 1995/96 season proved a year of consolidation in the 1st Division for Mark Bowen and his colleagues. Off the field, however, life was not straightforward with the club having to compensate Bradford City following the appointment of Gary Megson as manager and, in the build up to the new season, the appointment of a new Chairman after the departure of the controversial Robert Chase. The new season sees Mike Walker back in charge; Canaries' fans will be hoping that he will be able to bring back the good times to Carrow Road.

# NOTTINGHAM FOREST

## City Ground, Nottingham, NG2 5FJ

**Tel No:** 0115 952 6000
**Advance Tickets Tel No:** 0115 952 6002
**League:** F.A. Premier
**Brief History:** Founded 1865 as Forest Football Club, changed name to Nottingham Forest (c.1879). Former Grounds: Forest Recreation Ground, Meadow Cricket Ground, Trent Bridge (Cricket Ground), Parkside, Gregory Ground & Town Ground, moved to City Ground in 1898. Founder-members of Second Division (1892). Record attendance 49,045.

**(Total) Current capacity:** 30,500 (all seated)
**Visiting Supporters' Allocation:** Approx 4,800
**Club Colours:** Red shirts, white shorts
**Nearest Railway Station:** Nottingham Midland
**Parking (Car):** East car park & street parking
**Parking (Coach/Bus):** East car park
**Police Force and Tel No:** Nottinghamshire (0115 948 1888)
**Disabled Visitors' Facilities**
    **Wheelchairs:** Front of Executive Stand
    **Blind:** No special facility

*KEY*

**C** Club Offices
**S** Club Shop
**E** Entrance(s) for visiting supporters

↑ North direction (approx)

❶ Radcliffe Road
❷ Lady Bay Bridge Road
❸ Trent Bridge
❹ Trent Bridge Cricket Ground
❺ Notts County F.C.
❻ River Trent
❼ Nottingham Midland BR Station (¹/₂ mile)

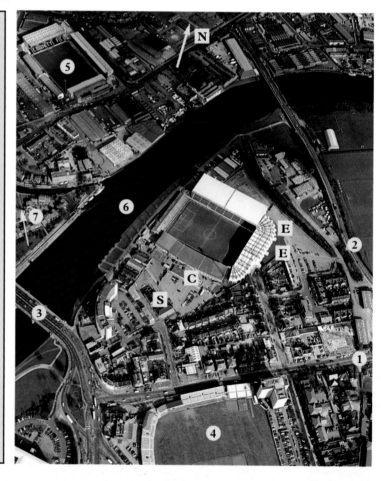

116

*Left:*
Lynchpin for the defence with both Forest and England, Stuart Pearce remains an influential figure for Frank Clark's team. He is another player whose reputation was considerably enhanced following strong performances in Euro '96; in particular he drew much credit for taking one of the penalties during the quarter final penalty shoot out against the Spanish.

# NOTTS COUNTY

## Meadow Lane, Nottingham, NG2 3HJ

**Tel No:** 0115 952 9000

**Advance Tickets Tel No:** 0115 955 7210

**League:** 2nd Division

**Brief History:** Founded 1862 (oldest club in Football League) as Nottingham, changed to Notts County in c.1882. Former Grounds: Notts Cricket Ground (Beeston), Castle Cricket Ground, Trent Bridge Cricket Ground, moved to Meadow Lane in 1910. Founder-members Football League (1888). Record attendance 47,310.

**(Total) Current Capacity:** 20,380 (seated)

**Visiting Supporters' Allocation:** 5,438 (seated)

**Club Colours:** Black & white striped shirts, white shorts.

**Nearest Railway Station:** Nottingham Midland

**Parking (Car):** Mainly street parking

**Parking (Coach/Bus):** Cattle market

**Police Force and Tel No:** Nottingham (0115 948 1888)

**Disabled Visitors' Facilities**
 **Wheelchairs:** Meadow Lane/Jimmy Sirrel/Derek Pavis Stands.
 **Blind:** No special facility

### KEY

**C** Club Offices

**S** Club Shop

**E** Entrance(s) for visiting supporters

**R** Refreshment bars for visiting supporters

**T** Toilets for visiting supporters

↑ North direction (approx)

❶ A6011 Meadow Lane
❷ County Road
❸ A60 London Road
❹ River Trent
❺ Nottingham Midland BR Station (1/2 mile)

*Right:*
Following their relegation, Notts County had the opportunity like Swindon to bounce straight back to the 2nd Division. Unfortunately for Shaun Murphy and his colleagues, County were outplayed in the 2nd Division Play-Off final and will have to be content with a further season in the 2nd Division.

# OLDHAM ATHLETIC

## Boundary Park, Oldham, OL1 2PA

**Tel No:** 0161 624 4972
**Advance Tickets Tel No:** 0161 624 4972
**League:** 1st Division
**Brief History:** Founded 1897 as Pine Villa, changed name to Oldham Athletic in 1899. Former Grounds: Berry's Field, Pine Mill, Athletic Ground (later named Boundary Park), Hudson Fold, moved to Boundary Park in 1906. Record attendance 47,671.
**(Total) Current Capacity:** 13,500 (all seated)
**Visiting Supporters' Allocation:** 1,500 minimum, 5,000 maximum
**Club Colours:** Blue and red shirts, white shorts

**Nearest Railway Station:** Oldham Werneth
**Parking (Car):** Lookers Stand car park
**Parking (Coach/Bus):** At Ground
**Police Force and Tel No:** Greater Manchester (0161 624 0444)
**Disabled Visitors' Facilities**
   **Wheelchairs:** Rochdale Road and Seton Stands
   **Blind:** No special facility
**Anticipated Development(s):** A new stand is planned to replace the existing Lookers Stand. This will increase capacity at the ground to some 23,000 when completed.

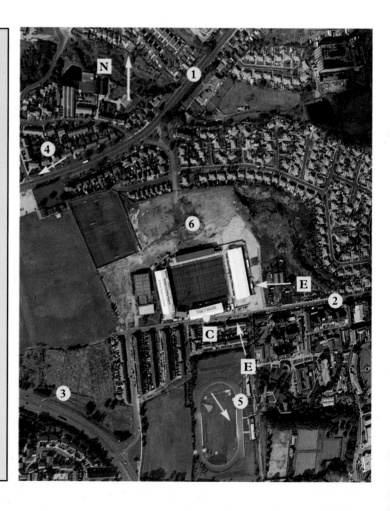

**KEY**

**C**  Club Offices
**E**  Entrance(s) for visiting supporters

↑  North direction (approx)

❶  A663 Broadway
❷  Furtherwood Road
❸  Chadderton Way
❹  To A627(M) and M62
❺  To Oldham Werneth BR Station (1½ miles)
❻  Car Park

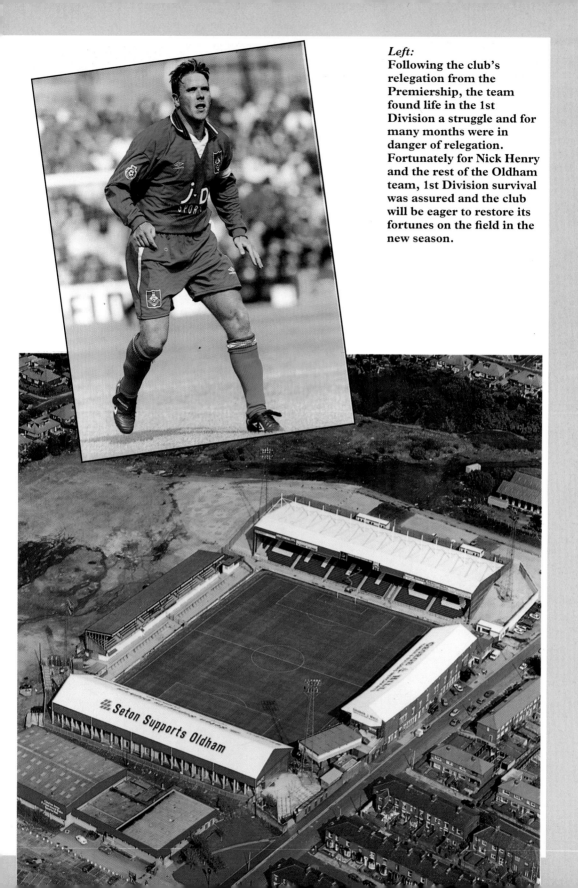

*Left:*
Following the club's relegation from the Premiership, the team found life in the 1st Division a struggle and for many months were in danger of relegation. Fortunately for Nick Henry and the rest of the Oldham team, 1st Division survival was assured and the club will be eager to restore its fortunes on the field in the new season.

Seton Supports Oldham

# OXFORD UNITED

## Manor Ground, London Road, Headington, Oxford, OX3 7RS

**Tel No:** 01865 61503
**Advance Tickets Tel No:** 01865 61503
**League:** 1st Division
**Brief History:** Founded 1893 as Headington
(later Headington United), changed name to
Oxford United in 1960. Former grounds:
Brittania Inn Field, Headington Quarry,
Wooten's Field, Manor Ground, The
Paddocks, moved back to Manor Ground in
1925. Record attendance 22,730.
**(Total) Current Capacity:** 9,572 (6,769 seated)
**Visiting Supporters' Allocation:** 2,649
**Club Colours:** Yellow with navy trim shirts, navy
with yellow trim shorts.

**Nearest Railway Station:** Oxford (3 miles)
**Parking (Car):** Street parking
**Parking (Coach/Bus):** Headley Way
**Police Force and Tel No:** Thames Valley
(01865 777501)
**Disabled Visitors' Facilities**
  **Wheelchairs:** Main Stand
  **Blind:** No special facility
**Anticipated Development(s):** Anticipated
move to new 15,000 capacity all-seated
stadium.

---

*KEY*
**C** Club Offices
**E** Entrance(s) for visiting
supporters
**R** Refreshment bars for visiting
supporters

↑ North direction (approx)

❶ A420 London Road
❷ Osler Road
❸ To City Centre and Oxford
BR Station (3 miles)
❹ To A40 and Ring Road
(¾ mile)
❺ Cuckoo Lane

*Right:*
**The 1995/96 season proved successful for Oxford United as the team snatched the second automatic promotion spot to the 1st Division from Blackpool right at the season's end. Here United's Matt Murphy is seen in FA Cup action on 13 February in the tie against Nottingham Forest.**

# PETERBOROUGH UNITED

## London Road, Peterborough, Cambs, PE2 8AL

**Tel No:** 01733 63947
**Advance Tickets Tel No:** 01733 63947
**League:** 2nd Division
**Brief History:** Founded in 1934, (no connection with former 'Peterborough and Fletton United' FC). Elected to Football League in 1960. Record attendance 30,096.
**(Total) Current Capacity:** 15,000 (9,800 seated)
**Visiting Supporters' Allocation:** 3,888 (888 seated)
**Club Colours:** Blue shirts, white shorts

**Nearest Railway Station:** Peterborough
**Parking (Car):** At ground
**Parking (Coach/Bus):** At ground
**Police Force and Tel No:** Cambridgeshire (01733 63232)
**Disabled Visitors' Facilities**
  **Wheelchairs:** London Road End
  **Blind:** Commentary available
**Future Development(s):** The next phase in the redevelopment of the ground, following the completion of the Freeman's Stand, will see the disappearance of the Moys End.

**KEY**
**C** Club Offices
**S** Club Shop
**E** Entrance(s) for visiting supporters
**R** Refreshment bars for visiting supporters
**T** Toilets for visiting supporters

↑ North direction (approx)

❶ A15 London Road
❷ Car Parks
❸ Peterborough BR Station (1 mile)
❹ Glebe Road
❺ A605
❻ To A1 (5 miles)

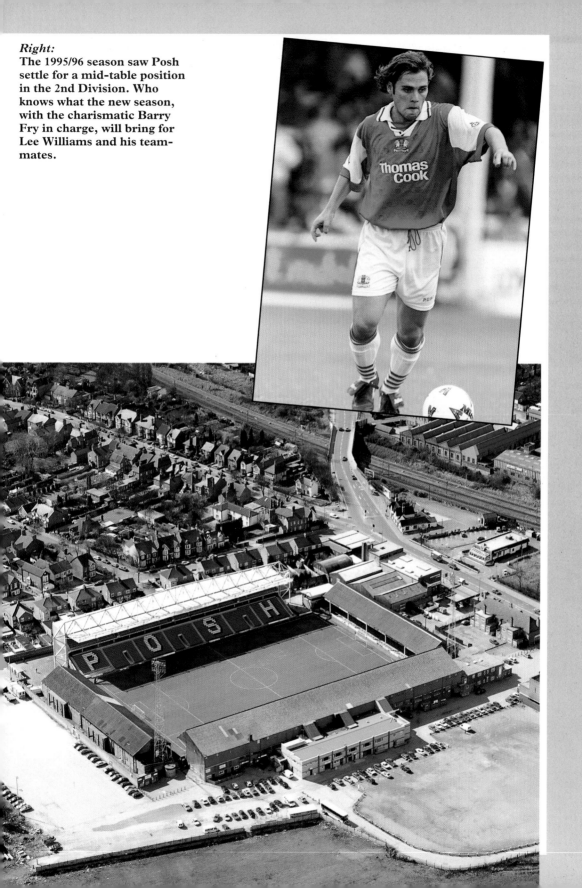

*Right:*
The 1995/96 season saw Posh settle for a mid-table position in the 2nd Division. Who knows what the new season, with the charismatic Barry Fry in charge, will bring for Lee Williams and his team-mates.

# PLYMOUTH ARGYLE

## Home Park, Plymouth, PL2 3DQ

**Tel No:** 01752 562561
**Advance Tickets Tel No:** 01752 562561
**League:** 2nd Division
**Brief History:** Founded 1886 as Argyle Athletic Club, changed name to Plymouth Argyle in 1903. Founder-members Third Division (1920). Record attendance 43,596
**(Total) Current Capacity:** 19,900 (8,800 seated)
**Visiting Supporters' Allocation:** 2,840
**Club Colours:** Green & white striped shirts, black shorts

**Nearest Railway Station:** Plymouth
**Parking (Car):** Car park adjacent
**Parking (Coach/Bus):** Central car park
**Police Force and Tel No:** Devon & Cornwall (01752 701188)
**Disabled Visitors' Facilities**
　**Wheelchairs:** Devonport End
　**Blind:** Commentary available
**Anticipated Development(s):** The club has plans to move to a new 23,000 all-seater stadium by the start of the 1998/99 season.

## KEY

**C** Club Offices
**S** Club Shop
**E** Entrance(s) for visiting supporters
**R** Refreshment bars for visiting supporters
**T** Toilets for visiting supporters

⬆ North direction (approx)

❶ Outland Road
❷ Car Park
❸ Devonport Road
❹ Central Park
❺ Town Centre & Plymouth BR Station (¾ mile)

*Left:*
**Pilgrims' keeper Nicky Hammond conducts his defence in August 1995. The 1995/96 season proved successful for Plymouth Argyle as promotion back to the 2nd Division was achieved through the 3rd Division Play-Off final.**

# PORTSMOUTH

## Fratton Park, 57 Frogmore Road, Portsmouth, Hants, PO4 8RA

**Tel No:** 01705 731204
**Advance Tickets Tel No:** 01705 618777
**League:** 1st Division
**Brief History:** Founded 1898. Founder-members Third Division (1920). Record attendance 51,385.
**(Total) Current Capacity:** 11,092 (all seated)
**Visiting Supporters' Allocation:** 1,720
**Club Colours:** Blue shirts, white shorts
**Nearest Railway Station:** Fratton
**Parking (Car):** Street parking
**Parking (Coach/Bus):** As directed by Police

**Police Force and Tel No:** Hampshire (01705 321111)
**Disabled Visitors' Facilities**
　**Wheelchairs:** Frogmore Road
　**Blind:** No special facility
**Anticipated Development(s):** Work will commence during the 1996/97 season on the building of the new Fratton Stand. This, combined with additional work next summer, will see the ground's capacity increased back to c19,000 for the start of the 1997/98 season.

### KEY

**C** Club Offices
**S** Club Shop
**E** Entrance(s) for visiting supporters
**R** Refreshment bars for visiting supporters
**T** Toilets for visiting supporters

↑ North direction (approx)

❶ Alverstone Road
❷ Carisbrook Road
❸ A288 Milton Road
❹ A2030 Eastern Road to A27
❺ A2030 Goldsmith Avenue
❻ Fratton BR Station (½ mile)

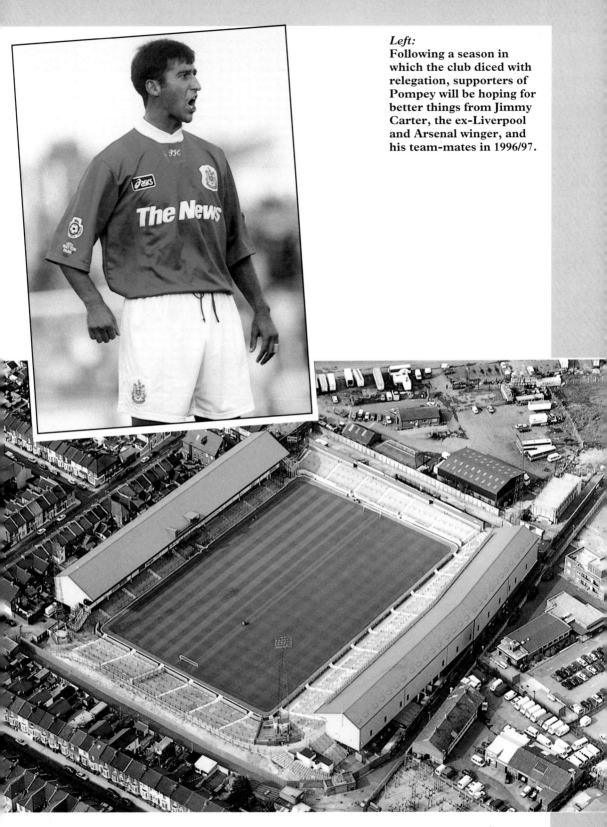

*Left:*
Following a season in which the club diced with relegation, supporters of Pompey will be hoping for better things from Jimmy Carter, the ex-Liverpool and Arsenal winger, and his team-mates in 1996/97.

# PORT VALE

## Vale Park, Burslem, Stoke-on-Trent, ST6 1AW

**Tel No:** 01782 814134
**Advance Tickets Tel No:** 01782 814134
**League:** 1st Division
**Brief History:** Founded 1876 as Burslem Port Vale, changed name to 'Port Vale' in 1907 (reformed club). Former Grounds: The Meadows Longport, Moorland Road Athletic Ground, Cobridge Athletic Grounds, Recreation Ground Hanley, moved to Vale Park in 1950. Founder-members Second Division (1892). Record attendance 50,000.
**(Total) Current Capacity:** 22,356 (17,616 seated)

**Visiting Supporters' Allocation:** 4,550
**Club Colours:** White shirts, black shorts
**Nearest Railway Station:** Stoke
**Parking (Car):** Car park at Ground
**Parking (Coach/Bus):** Hamil Road car park
**Police Force and Tel No:** Staffordshire (01782 577114)
**Disabled Visitors' Facilities**
    **Wheelchairs:** Specialist Stand - Lorne Street
    **Blind:** Commentary available

**KEY**

**C** Club Offices
**E** Entrance(s) for visiting supporters

↑ North direction (approx)

❶ Car Parks
❷ Hamil Road
❸ Lorne Street
❹ B5051 Moorland Road

130

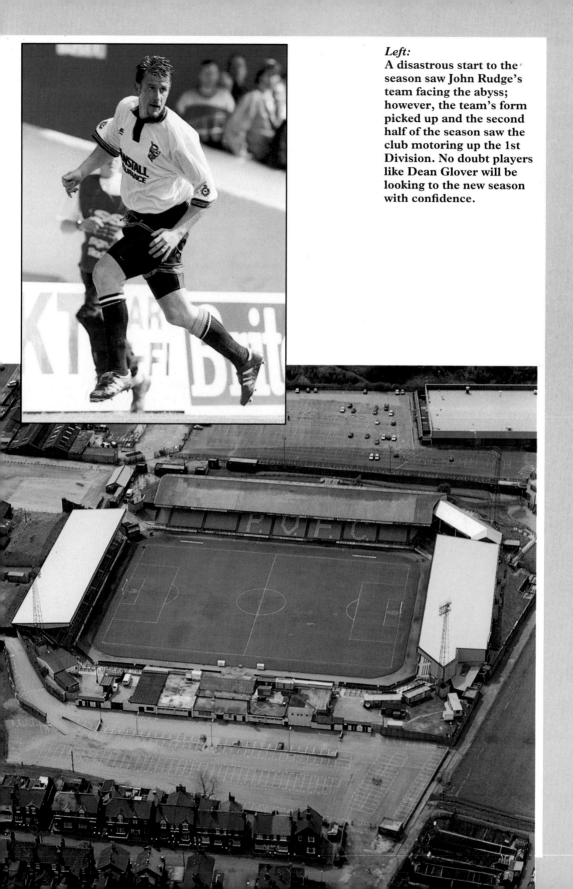

*Left:*
**A disastrous start to the season saw John Rudge's team facing the abyss; however, the team's form picked up and the second half of the season saw the club motoring up the 1st Division. No doubt players like Dean Glover will be looking to the new season with confidence.**

# PRESTON NORTH END

## Lowthorpe Road, Deepdale, PR1 6RU

**Tel No:** 01772 902020
**Advance Tickets Tel No:** 01772 902000
**League:** 2nd Division
**Brief History:** Founded 1867 as a Rugby Club, changed to soccer in 1881. Former ground: Moor park, moved to (later named) Deepdale in 1875. Founder-members Football League (1888). Record attendance 42,684.
**(Total) Current Capacity:** 18,000 (8,868 seated)
**Visiting Supporters' Allocation:** 650
**Club Colours:** White shirts, blue shorts
**Nearest Railway Station:** Preston (2 miles)

**Parking (Car):** West Stand car park
**Parking (Coach/Bus):** West Stand car park
**Police Force and Tel No:** Lancashire (01772 203203)
**Disabled Visitors' Facilities**
  **Wheelchairs:** Tom Finney Stand
  **Blind:** Earphones Commentary
**Anticipated Development(s):** With the completion of the dramatic Tom Finney stand (face *et al*), the next phase in the ground's redevelopment is likely to affect the Fulwood End.

*KEY*
**C** Club Offices
**S** Club Shop

⬆ North direction (approx)

❶ A6033 Deepdale Road
❷ Lawthorpe Road
❸ Car Park
❹ A5085 Blackpool Road
❺ Preston BR Station (2 miles)
❻ Fulwood End – Spion Kop
❼ Tom Finney Stand

A good season off and on the pitch saw Preston promoted to the 2nd Division and the completion of the Tom Finney Stand. Andy. Saville seems in quizzical mood during the league game on 4 May 1996.

# QUEENS PARK RANGERS

## Rangers Stadium, South Africa Road, London, W12 7PA

**Tel No:** 0181 743 0262
**Tickets and Info. Tel No:** 0181 740 0610
**League:** 1st Division
**Brief History:** Founded 1885 as 'St. Jude's Institute', amalgamated with Christchurch Rangers to become Queens Park Rangers in 1886. Football League record number of former Grounds and Ground moves (13 different venues, 17 changes), including White City Stadium (twice) final move to Rangers Stadium (then named Loftus Road) in 1963. Founder-members Third Division (1920). Record attendance 35,353.
**(Total) Current Capacity:** 19,074 (all seated)

**Visiting Supporters' Allocation:** 3,100
**Club Colours:** Blue & white hooped shirts, white shorts
**Nearest Railway Station:** Shepherds Bush and White City (both tube)
**Parking (Car):** White City NCP & street parking
**Parking (Coach/Bus):** White City NCP
**Police Force and Tel No:** Metropolitan (0181 246 2725)
**Disabled Visitors' Facilities**
  **Wheelchairs:** Ellerslie Road Stand & West Paddock
  **Blind:** Ellerslie Road Stand

**KEY**
- **C** Club Offices
- **S** Club Shop
- **E** Entrance(s) for visiting supporters

↑ North direction (approx)

❶ South Africa Road
❷ To White City Tube Station, A219 Wood Lane and A40 Western Avenue
❸ A4020 Uxbridge Road
❹ To Shepherds Bush Tube Station
❺ Ellerslie Road

*Left:*
Each season there is one team that, according to the pundits, is too good to get relegated. The unfortunate recipient of that accolade in the 1995/96 season was Ray Wilkins' Queens Park Rangers. Players like Trevor Sinclair produced a number of attractive performances, but the team's lack of consistency brought 1st Division football to Loftus Road for 1996/97.

# READING

## Elm Park, Norfolk Road, Reading, RG3 2EF

**Tel No:** 0118 950 7878

**Advance Tickets Tel No:** 0118 950 7878

**League:** 1st Division

**Brief History:** Founded 1871. (Amalgamated with Reading Hornets in 1877 and with Earley in 1889.) Former Grounds: Reading Recreation Ground, Reading Cricket Ground, Coley Park and Caversham Cricket Ground, moved to Elm Park in 1895. Founder-members Third Division (1920). Record attendance 33,042.

**(Total) Current Capacity:** 14,058 (2,242 seated)

**Visiting Supporters' Allocation:** 3,174 (342 seated)

**Club Colours:** White with blue hoops shirts, white shorts

**Nearest Railway Station:** Reading West

**Parking (Car):** Street parking & Park & Ride scheme from Prospect School, Honey End Lane.

**Parking (Coach/Bus):** The Meadway

**Police Force and Tel No:** Thames Valley (01734 536000)

**Disabled Visitors' Facilities**

**Wheelchairs:** Norfolk Road

**Blind:** Organised by Hospital Radio

**Anticipated Development(s):** The club is planning to relocate to a new 25,000 all-seater stadium at Smallmead for the start of the 1997/98 season.

---

### KEY

**C** Club Offices

**S** Club Shop

**E** Entrance(s) for visiting supporters

**R** Refreshment bars for visiting supporters

**T** Toilets for visiting supporters

↑ North direction (approx)

❶ Tilehurst Road

❷ Norfolk Road

❸ County Cricket Ground

❹ Reading West BR Station (½ mile)

❺ Liebenrood Road to A4 Bath Road (¼ mile)

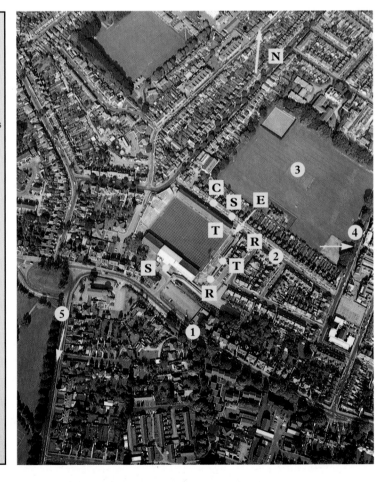

**Left:**
Like Brentford, Reading seems to have suffered after effects following defeat in the 1994/95 Play-Off Finals. Last season the team rarely achieved the form that had made it appear a good bet for promotion the previous year — and that was despite the efforts of high-profile supporter Uri Geller. The Royals' Lee Nogan concentrates on giving the ball (and the club) a lift.

# ROCHDALE

## Willbutts Lane, Spotland, Rochdale, OL11 5DS

**Tel No:** 01706 44648
**Advance Tickets Tel No:** 01706 44648
**League:** 3rd Division
**Brief History:** Founded 1907 from former Rochdale Town F.C. (founded 1900). Founder-members Third Division North (1921). Record attendance 24,231.
**(Total) Current Capacity:** 6,448 (2,054 seated)
**Visiting Supporters' Allocation:** 2,700 (700 seated)
**Club Colours:** Blue & white shirts, white shorts
**Nearest Railway Station:** Rochdale

**Parking (Car):** Rear of ground
**Parking (Coach/Bus):** Rear of ground
**Police Force and Tel No:** Greater Manchester (01706 47401)
**Disabled Visitors' Facilities**
**Wheelchairs:** Main stand - disabled area
**Blind:** Commentary available
**Anticipated Development(s):** Work has started on the new Pear Street Stand. This 2,600-seat stand will increase the ground's capacity to over 9,000.

**KEY**

- **C** Club Offices
- **S** Club Shop
- **E** Entrance(s) for visiting supporters
- **R** Refreshment bars for visiting supporters
- **T** Toilets for visiting supporters

↑ North direction (approx)

❶ Willbutts Lane
❷ A627 Edenfield Road
❸ Rochdale BR Station (¹/₂ mile)
❹ Sandy Lane

# ROTHERHAM UNITED

## Millmoor Ground, Rotherham, S60 1HR

**Tel No:** 01709 512434
**Advance Tickets Tel No:** 01709 512434
**League:** 2nd Division
**Brief History:** Founded 1877 (as Thornhill, later Thornhill United), changed name to Rotherham County in 1905 and to Rotherham United in 1925, (amalgamated with Rotherham Town - Football League members 1893-97 - in 1925). Former Grounds include: Red House Ground & Clifton Lane Cricket Ground, moved to Millmoor in 1907. Record attendance 25,000.
**(Total) Current Capacity:** 11,489 (4,442 seated)

**Visiting Supporters' Allocation:** 4,219 (1,094 seated)
**Club Colours:** Red shirts, white shorts
**Nearest Railway Station:** Rotherham Central
**Parking (Car):** Kimberworth and Main Street car parks, plus large car park adjacent to ground.
**Parking (Coach/Bus):** As directed by Police
**Police Force and Tel No:** South Yorkshire (01709 371121)
**Disabled Visitors' Facilities**
  **Wheelchairs:** Millmoor Lane
  **Blind:** No special facility

---

**KEY**

**C** Club Offices
**S** Club Shop
**E** Entrance(s) for visiting supporters
**R** Refreshment bars for visiting supporters
**T** Toilets for visiting supporters

↑ North direction (approx)

❶ Car Park
❷ Rotherham Central BR Station
❸ A6109 Masborough Road
❹ Millmoor Lane
❺ To A6178 and M1 Junction 34

*Left:*
**Shaun Goater's success as a striker continues to bring him to the attention of bigger clubs.**

# SCARBOROUGH

## McCain Stadium, Seamer Road, Scarborough, N. Yorkshire YO12 4HF

**Tel No:** 01723 375094
**Advance Tickets Tel No:** 01723 375094
**League:** 3rd Division
**Brief History:** Founded 1879 as 'Scarborough Cricketers F.C.' changed name to 'Scarborough F.C.' in 1887. Former grounds: North Marine (Cricket) Ground and Recreation Ground, moved to (then named) Athletic Ground in 1898. Promoted to Football League in 1987. Record attendance 11,124.
**(Total) Current Capacity:** 6,230 (3,379 seated)
**Visiting Supporters' Allocation:** 1,336 (all seated)

**Club Colours:** Red shirts, black shorts
**Nearest Railway Station:** Scarborough Central (2 miles)
**Parking (Car):** Street parking
**Parking (Coach/Bus):** Weaponess coach/car park
**Police Force and Tel No:** North Yorkshire (01723 500300)
**Disabled Visitors' Facilities**
  **Wheelchairs:** Main Stand, Edgehill Road end.
  **Blind:** No special facility

### KEY

**C** Club Offices
**E** Entrance(s) for visiting supporters
**R** Refreshment bars for visiting supporters
**T** Toilets for visiting supporters

↑ North direction (approx)

**❶** A64 Seamer Road
**❷** Scarborough Central BR Station (2 miles)
**❸** To York
**❹** McCain Stand

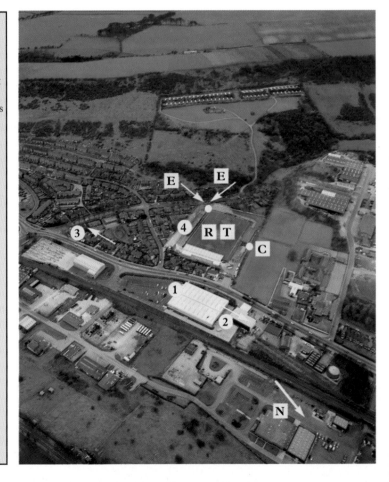

*Left:*
**Boro's Andy Toman keeps a wary out for the opposition in this 3rd Division clash with Gillingham on 4 May 1996.**

# SCUNTHORPE UNITED

## Glanford Park, Doncaster Road, Scunthorpe DN15 8TD

**Tel No:** 01724 848077
**Advance Tickets Tel No:** 01724 848077
**League:** 3rd Division
**Brief History:** Founded 1899 as Scunthorpe United, amalgamated with North Lindsey to become 'Scunthorpe & Lindsey United in 1912. Changed name to Scunthorpe United in 1956. Former grounds: Crosby (Lindsey United) & Old Showground, moved to Glanford Park in 1988. Elected to Football League in 1950. Record attendance 8,775 (23,935 at Old Showground).

**(Total) Current Capacity:** 9,200 (6,400 seated)
**Visiting Supporters' Allocation:** 1,678
**Club Colours:** Sky blue shirts with two claret rings on sleeves, white shorts with claret stripe.
**Nearest Railway Station:** Scunthorpe
**Parking (Car):** At ground
**Parking (Coach/Bus):** At ground
**Police Force and Tel No:** Humberside (01724 282888)
**Disabled Visitors' Facilities**
  **Wheelchairs:** Clugston Stand
  **Blind:** Commentary available

*KEY*
**C** Club Offices
**S** Club Shop
**E** Entrance(s) for visiting supporters
**R** Refreshment bars for visiting supporters
**T** Toilets for visiting supporters

↑ North direction (approx)

❶ Car Park
❷ Glanford Stand
❸ A18 Scunthorpe BR Station and Town Centre (1½ miles)
❹ M181 and M180 Junction 3

*Left:*
**Irons' John Eyre comes forward with the ball in this 1 January 1996 3rd Division encounter.**

# SHEFFIELD UNITED

## Bramall Lane, Sheffield, S2 4SU

**Tel No:** 0114 273 8955
**Advance Tickets Tel No:** 0114 276 6771
**League:** 1st Division
**Brief History:** Founded 1889. (Sheffield Wednesday occasionally used Bramall Lane c.1880). Founder-members 2nd Division (1892). Record attendance 68,287
**(Total) Current Capacity:** 23,390 (all seated)
**Visiting Supporters' Allocation:** 2,000 (seated)
**Club Colours:** Red & white striped shirts, black shorts
**Nearest Railway Station:** Sheffield Midland

**Parking (Car):** Street parking
**Parking (Coach/Bus):** As directed by Police
**Police Force and Tel No:** South Yorkshire (0114 276 8522)
**Disabled Visitors' Facilities**
  **Wheelchairs:** John Street South Stand
  **Blind:** Commentary available
**Anticipated Development(s):** Construction started in the summer of 1996 on the new John Street Stand. When completed, this will raise the ground's capacity to 30,000.

---

**KEY**

**C** Club Offices
**E** Entrance(s) for visiting supporters
**R** Refreshment bars for visiting supporters
**T** Toilets for visiting supporters

↑ North direction (approx)

❶ A621 Bramall Lane
❷ Shoreham Street
❸ Car Park
❹ Sheffield Midland BR Station (¼ mile)
❺ John Street
❻ Spion Kop
❼ John Street Stand (under construction)

**Left:**
Like Norwich City, Sheffield
United struggled to find form
following their relegation to the
1st Division and parted
company with manager Dave
Bassett during the season. Dane
Whitehouse appears to be
looking over his shoulder for
further trouble in January 1996
shot; fortunately for him and
the team, the club's form
improved and the team staved
off a second successive
relegation. With Howard
Kendall now in charge, fans will
have high expectations for the
1996/97 season.

# SHEFFIELD WEDNESDAY

## Hillsborough, Sheffield, S6 1SW

**Tel No:** 0114 221 2121

**Advance Tickets Tel No:** 0114 221 2400

**League:** F.A. Premier

**Brief History:** Founded 1867 as The Wednesday F.C. (changed to Sheffield Wednesday c.1930). Former Grounds: London Road, Wyrtle Road (Heeley), Sheaf House Ground, Encliffe & Olive Grove (Bramall Lane also used occasionally), moved to Hillsborough (then named 'Owlerton' in 1899). Founder-members Second Division (1892). Record attendance 72,841.

**(Total) Current Capacity:** 39,500 (all seated)

**Visiting Supporters' Allocation:** 4,193 (all seated)

**Club Colours:** Blue & white striped shirts, blue shorts

**Nearest Railway Station:** Sheffield (4 miles)

**Parking (Car):** Street Parking

**Parking (Coach/Bus):** Owlerton Stadium

**Police Force and Tel No:** South Yorkshire (0114 234 3131)

**Disabled Visitors' Facilities**
  **Wheelchairs:** North Stand
  **Blind:** Commentary available

*KEY*
- **C** Club Offices
- **S** Club Shop
- **E** Entrance(s) for visiting supporters

↑ North direction (approx)

❶ Leppings Lane
❷ River Dom
❸ A61 Penistone Road North
❹ Sheffield BR Station and City Centre (4 miles)
❺ Spion Kop
❻ To M1 (North)
❼ To M1 (South)

*Left:*
One of the few — the only? Can you name four other famous Belgian footballers playing in England? — Belgians with an English club, Marc Degryse and the rest of David Pleat's team suffered a disappointing 1995/96 season, which almost saw the club sucked into the relegation quagmire.

# SHREWSBURY TOWN

## Gay Meadow, Shrewsbury, SY2 6AB

**Tel No:** 01743 360111
**Advance Tickets Tel No:** 01743 360111
**League:** 2nd Division
**Brief History:** Founded 1886. Former Grounds: Monkmoor Racecourse, Ambler's Field & The Barracks Ground (moved to Gay Meadow in 1910). Elected to Football League in 1950. Record attendance 18,917
**(Total) Current Capacity:** 8,000 (3,500 seated)
**Visiting Supporters' Allocation:** 2,000
**Club Colours:** Blue with White collar shirts, blue shorts.

**Nearest Railway Station:** Shrewsbury
**Parking (Car):** Adjacent car park
**Parking (Coach/Bus):** Gay Meadow
**Police Force and Tel No:** West Mercia (01743 232888)
**Disabled Visitors' Facilities**
  **Wheelchairs:** Alongside Pitch (as directed)
  **Blind:** No special facility
**Anticipated Development(s):** If vague talk of a relocation comes to nothing, then the club will redevelop Gay Meadow.

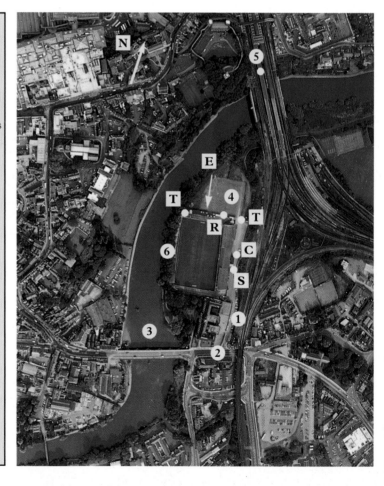

### KEY

**C** Club Offices
**S** Club Shop
**E** Entrance(s) for visiting supporters
**R** Refreshment bars for visiting supporters
**T** Toilets for visiting supporters

↑ North direction (approx)

❶ Entrance road to ground
❷ Abbey Foregate
❸ River Severn
❹ Car Parks
❺ Shrewsbury BR Station (1 mile — shortest route)
❻ Riverside enclosure

**Right:**
After a good start to the new season following their promotion, the Shrews' form deteriorated after Christmas and the team gradually sank down the table. The season's highpoint for Mark Dempsey and his colleagues was, however, a trip to Wembley — the first in the club's history — when the team met Rotherham in the final of the Auto-Windscreen Trophy.

# SOUTHAMPTON

## The Dell, Milton Road, Southampton, SO15 2XH

**Tel No:** 01703 220505
**Advance Tickets Tel No:** 01703 228575
**League:** F.A. Premier
**Brief History:** Founded 1885 as 'Southampton St. Mary's Young Mens Association' (changed name to Southampton in 1897). Former Grounds: Northlands Road, Antelope Ground, County Ground, moved to The Dell in 1898. Founder-members Third Division (1920). Record attendance 31,044.
**(Total) Current Capacity:** 15,000 (all seated)
**Visiting Supporters' Allocation:** 1,500 (all seated)

**Club Colours:** Red & white shirts, black shorts
**Nearest Railway Station:** Southampton
**Parking (Car):** Street parking
**Parking (Coach/Bus):** As directed by Police
**Police Force and Tel No:** Hampshire (01703 581111)
**Disabled Visitors' Facilities**
  **Wheelchairs:** Milton Road (book in advance)
  **Blind:** Commentary available (book in advance)

---

### KEY
**C** Club Offices
**S** Club Shop
**E** Entrance(s) for visiting supporters
**R** Refreshment bars for visiting supporters
**T** Toilets for visiting supporters

⬆ North direction (approx)

❶ Archers Road
❷ Milton Road
❸ Hill Lane
❹ To Southampton BR station
❺ To A33, M3 and the north

Southampton had a disappointing 1995/96 season, flirting with relegation until the last game. One factor in this was the variable form of Matthew le Tissier (right); on the one hand he showed the stunning form that brought him to the fringes of the England squad, on the other there were occasions when he was almost anonymous. The arrival of Graham Souness to the Southampton managership promises an interesting season at the Dell.

# SOUTHEND UNITED

## Roots Hall Ground, Victoria Avenue, Southend-on-Sea, SS2 6NQ

**Tel No:** 01702 304050
**Advance Tickets Tel No:** 01702 304090
**League:** 1st Division
**Brief History:** Founded 1906. Former Grounds: Roots Hall, Kursaal, The Stadium Grainger Road, moved to Roots Hall (new Ground) 1955. Founder-members Third Division (1920). Record attendance 31,033.
**(Total) Current Capacity:** 12,500 (all seated)
**Visiting Supporters' Allocation:** 2,400 (increasing to a maximum of 3,100) in the North Stand.

**Club Colours:** Blue shirts, blue shorts
**Nearest Railway Station:** Prittlewell
**Parking (Car):** Street parking
**Parking (Coach/Bus):** Car park at Ground
**Police Force and Tel No:** Essex (01702 431212)
**Disabled Visitors' Facilities**
　**Wheelchairs:** West Stand
　**Blind:** Commentary available

### KEY

**C** Club Offices
**E** Entrance(s) for visiting supporters

↑ North direction (approx)

❶ Director's Car Park
❷ Prittlewell BR Station (¼ mile)
❸ A127 Victoria Avenue
❹ Fairfax Drive
❺ Southend centre (½ mile)
❻ North Bank

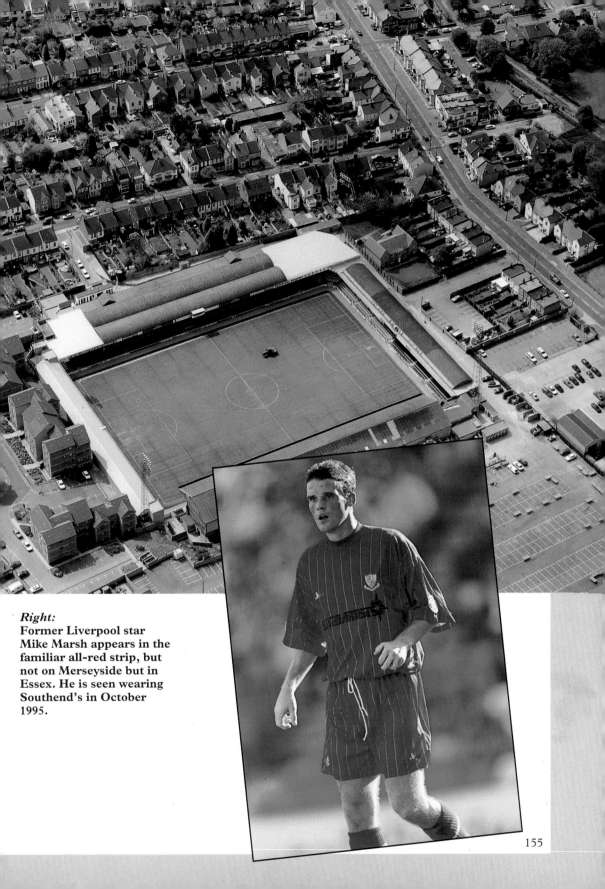

*Right:*
**Former Liverpool star Mike Marsh appears in the familiar all-red strip, but not on Merseyside but in Essex. He is seen wearing Southend's in October 1995.**

# STOCKPORT COUNTY

## Edgeley Park, Hardcastle Road, Edgeley, Stockport, SK3 9DD

**Tel No:** 0161 286 8888
**Advance Tickets Tel No:** 0161 286 8888
**League:** 2nd Division
**Brief History:** Founded 1883 as Heaton Norris Rovers, changed name to Stockport County in 1890. Former Grounds: Heaton Norris Recreation Ground, Heaton Norris Wanderers Cricket Ground, Chorlton's Farm, Ash Inn Ground, Wilkes Field (Belmont Street) and Nursery Inn (Green Lane), moved to Edgeley Park in 1902. Record attendance 27,833.
**(Total) Current Capacity:** 12,160 (9,410 seated)
**Visiting Supporters' Allocation:** 3,400

**Club Colours:** Blue shirts with red & white flashes, white shorts
**Nearest Railway Station:** Stockport
**Parking (Car):** Street parking
**Parking (Coach/Bus):** As directed by Police
**Police Force and Tel No:** Greater Manchester (0161 872 5050)
**Disabled Visitors' Facilities**
**Wheelchairs:** Main Stand
**Blind:** Headsets available
**Anticipated Development(s):** The Cheadle Stand was completed during the 1995/96 season. Apart from reseating the Main Stand nothing else is planned.

**KEY**

**C** Club Offices
**E** Entrance(s) for visiting supporters

↑ North direction (approx)

❶ Mercian Way
❷ Hardcastle Road
❸ Stockport BR Station (¼ mile)
❹ Railway End
❺ Main Stand
❻ Cheadle Stand

*Left:*
**Sean Connelly of County seen in action on 21 October 1995. The 1995/96 season saw County on the fringes of the promotion race, with the team just failing to make a Play-Off spot. No doubt the Hatters will be amongst the favourites for success in the 2nd Division in 1996/97.**

# STOKE CITY

## Victoria Ground, Boothen Old Road, Stoke-on-Trent, ST4 4EG

**Tel No:** 01782 413511
**Advance Tickets Tel No:** 01782 413961
**League:** 1st Division
**Brief History:** Founded 1863 as Stoke F.C., amalgamated with Stoke Victoria in 1878, changed to Stoke City in 1925. Former Ground: Sweetings Field, moved to Victoria Ground in 1878. Founder-members Football League (1888). Record attendance 51,380.
**(Total) Current Capacity:** Approx. 24,000 (approx. 9,000 seated)
**Visiting Supporters' Allocation:** Approx. 3,000
**Club Colours:** Red & white striped shirts, white shorts

**Nearest Railway Station:** Stoke-on-Trent
**Parking (Car):** Car park at ground
**Parking (Coach/Bus):** Whieldon Road
**Police Force and Tel No:** Staffordshire (01784 744644)
**Disabled Visitors' Facilities**
   **Wheelchairs:** Corner Butler Street/Boothen End
   **Blind:** Limited facilities (contact first)
**Anticipated Development(s):** The club has announced plans to move to a new 25,000 all-seater stadium for the start of the 1997/98 season.

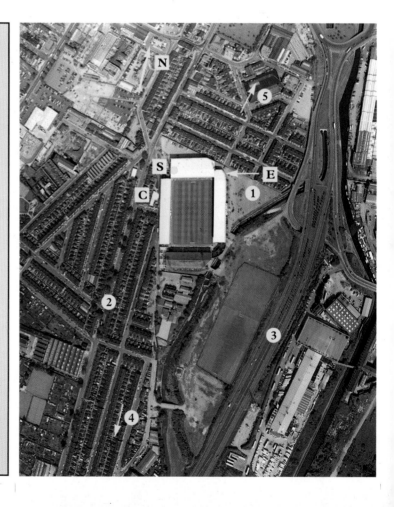

**KEY**
- **C** Club Offices
- **S** Club Shop
- **E** Entrance(s) for visiting supporters

↑ North direction (approx)

- ❶ Car Park
- ❷ Campbell Road
- ❸ A500 Queensway
- ❹ M6 Junction 15 (4 miles via A500)
- ❺ Stoke-on-Trent BR Station (½ mile)

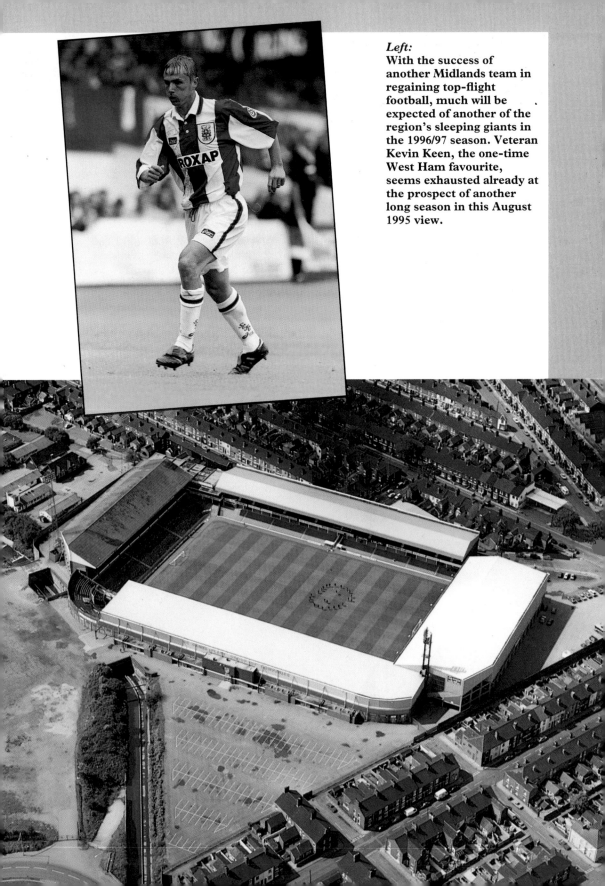

*Left:*
With the success of another Midlands team in regaining top-flight football, much will be expected of another of the region's sleeping giants in the 1996/97 season. Veteran Kevin Keen, the one-time West Ham favourite, seems exhausted already at the prospect of another long season in this August 1995 view.

# SUNDERLAND

## Roker Park, Grantham Road, Roker, Sunderland, SR6 9SW

**Tel No:** 0191 514 0332

**Advance Tickets Tel No:** 0191 514 0332

**League:** F. A. Premier

**Brief History:** Founded 1879 as 'Sunderland and District Teachers Association', changed to 'Sunderland Association' (in 1880) and shortly after to 'Sunderland'. Former Grounds: Blue House Field, Groves Field (Ashbrooke), Horatio Street, Abbs Field & Newcastle Road, moved to Roker Park in 1898. Record attendance 75,118

**(Total) Current Capacity:** 22,657 (7,811 seated)

**Visiting Supporters' Allocation:** Maximum of 3,399

**Club Colours:** Red & white striped shirts, black shorts

**Nearest Railway Station:** Seaburn

**Parking (Car):** Car park adjacent ground

**Parking (Coach/Bus):** Seafront, Roker

**Police Force and Tel No:** Northumbria (0191 567 6155)

**Disabled Visitors' Facilities**
  **Wheelchairs:** Roker Baths Road
  **Blind:** Commentary available

**Anticipated Development(s):** The club is proposing to build a new 34,000 all-seater stadium to replace Roker Park by the start of the 1997/98 season.

---

### KEY
**C** Club Offices
**S** Club Shop
**E** Entrance(s) for visiting supporters

↑ North direction (approx)

❶ Roker Baths Road
❷ Grantham Road
❸ Seaburn BR Station (1 mile)
❹ To A1018 Newcastle Road
❺ Hampden Road
❻ To A183 Roker Terrace (Seafront)
❼ Car Park

160

*Left:*
**Success in the 1st Division means that Sunderland's last season at Roker Park will be played at the highest level. The Manchester City connection, with Peter Reid as manager, is also exemplified by veteran Paul Bracewell playing on Wearside.**

# SWANSEA CITY

## Vetch Field, Swansea, SA1 3SU

**Tel No:** 01792 474114

**Advance Tickets Tel No:** 01792 474114

**League:** 3rd Division

**Brief History:** Founded 1900 as Swansea Town, changed to Swansea City in 1970. Former Grounds: various, including Recreation Ground. Moved to Vetch Field in 1912. Founder-members Third Division (1920). Record attendance 32,796.

**(Total) Current Capacity:** 16,419 (3,414 seated)

**Visiting Supporters' Allocation:** 3,500

**Club Colours:** White shirts, white shorts

**Nearest Railway Station:** Swansea High Street

**Parking (Car):** Kingsway car park & adjacent Clarence Terrace, (supervised car park).

**Parking (Coach/Bus):** As directed by Police

**Police Force and Tel No:** South Wales (01792 456999)

**Disabled Visitors' Facilities**
**Wheelchairs:** Glamorgan Street
**Blind:** No special facility

**Anticipated Development(s):** There are tentative plans for relocation, but nothing has been confirmed.

**KEY**
- **C** Club Offices
- **S** Club Shop
- **E** Entrance(s) for visiting supporters

↑ North direction (approx)

- ❶ Glamorgan Street
- ❷ William Street
- ❸ Richardson Street
- ❹ A4067 Oystermouth Road (8 miles to M4 Junction 42)
- ❺ Swansea High Street BR Station (1/2 mile)
- ❻ Supervised Car Park
- ❼ North Bank

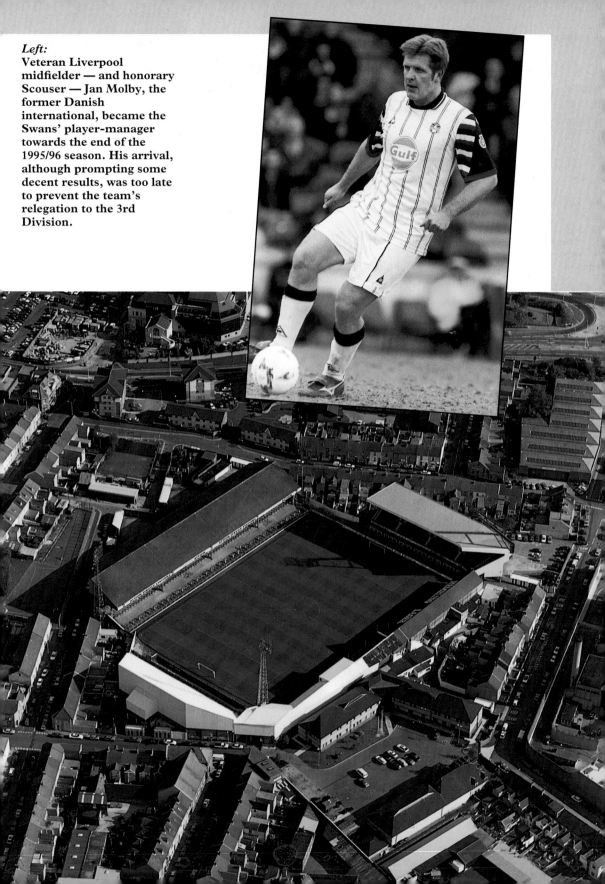

*Left:*
**Veteran Liverpool midfielder — and honorary Scouser — Jan Molby, the former Danish international, became the Swans' player-manager towards the end of the 1995/96 season. His arrival, although prompting some decent results, was too late to prevent the team's relegation to the 3rd Division.**

# SWINDON TOWN

## County Ground, County Road, Swindon, SN1 2ED

**Tel No:** 01793 430430
**Advance Tickets Tel No:** 01793 430430
**League:** 1st Division
**Brief History:** Founded 1881. Former Grounds: Quarry Ground, Globe Field, Croft Ground, County Ground (adjacent current to Ground and now Cricket Ground), moved to current County Ground in 1896. Founder-members Third Division (1920). Record attendance 32,000
**(Total) Current Capacity:** 15,700 (all seated)
**Visiting Supporters' Allocation:** 2,100 (all seated)

**Club Colours:** Red shirts, red shorts
**Nearest Railway Station:** Swindon
**Parking (Car):** Town Centre
**Parking (Coach/Bus):** Adjacent car park
**Police Force and Tel No:** Wiltshire (01793 528111)
**Disabled Visitors' Facilities**
  **Wheelchairs:** Intel Stand
  **Blind:** Commentary available
**Anticipated Development(s):** The next phase of work at the County Ground will be the construction of a 2,000 seat stand on the site of the Stratton Bank.

### KEY

**C** Club Offices
**S** Club Shop
**E** Entrance(s) for visiting supporters
**R** Refreshment bars for visiting supporters
**T** Toilets for visiting supporters

↑ North direction (approx)

❶ Shrivenham Road
❷ County Road
❸ A345 Queens Drive (M4 Junction 15 – 3½ miles)
❹ Swindon BR Station (½ mile)
❺ Town End
❻ Car Park
❼ County Cricket Ground
❽ Intel Stand
❾ Castrol Stand

*Right:*
**After the traumas of two consecutive relegations, the 1995/96 season was one of triumph as the Robins bounced back to the 1st Division at the first attempt. Shaun Taylor and his team-mates were a class apart from the rest of the 2nd Division and took the Championship in style.**

# TORQUAY UNITED

## Plainmoor Ground, Torquay, TQ1 3PS

**Tel No:** 01803 328666
**Advance Tickets Tel No:** 01803 328666
**League:** 3rd Division
**Brief History:** Founded 1898, as Torquay United, amalgamated with Ellacombe in 1910, changed name to Torquay Town. Amalgamated with Babbacombe in 1921, changed name to Torquay United. Former grounds: Teignmouth Road, Torquay Recreation Ground, Cricketfield Road & Torquay Cricket Ground, moved to Plainmoor (Ellacombe Ground) in 1910. Record attendance 21,908.
**(Total) Current Capacity:** 5,987 (2,324 seated)
**Visiting Supporters' Allocation:** 1,196 (200 seated)

**Club Colours:** Yellow with navy & white stripe shirts, navy shorts
**Nearest Railway Station:** Torquay (2 miles)
**Parking (Car):** Street parking
**Parking (Coach/Bus):** Lymington Road coach station
**Police Force and Tel No:** Devon & Cornwall (01803 214491)
**Disabled Visitors' Facilities**
  **Wheelchairs:** Ellacombe End
  **Blind:** Commentary available
**Anticipated Development(s):** The Babbacombe End, currently used by away supporters, is due to be replaced by a new 1,800 seat stand.

### KEY

**C** Club Offices
**S** Club Shop
**E** Entrance(s) for visiting supporters
**R** Refreshment bars for visiting supporters
**T** Toilets for visiting supporters

↑ North direction (approx)

❶ Warbro Road
❷ B3202 Marychurch Road
❸ Marnham Road
❹ Torquay BR Station (2 miles)

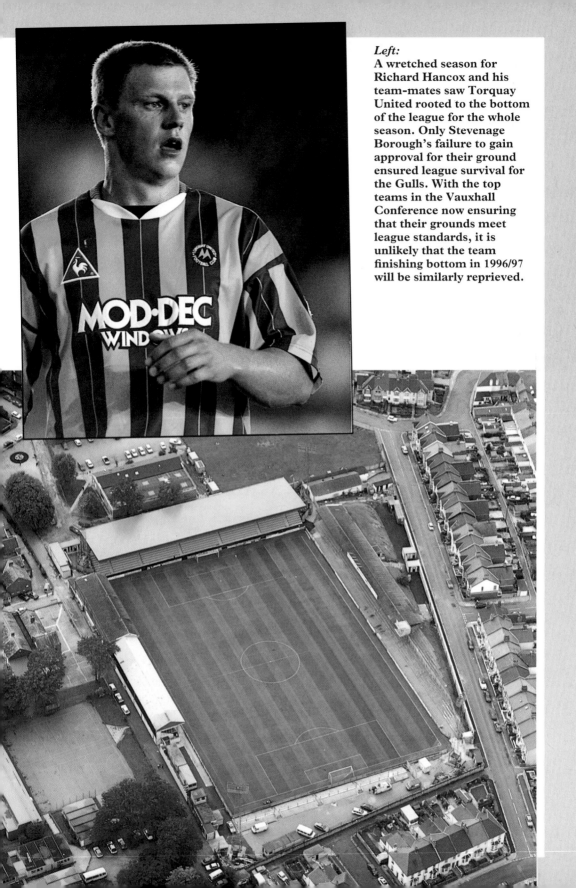

*Left:*
A wretched season for Richard Hancox and his team-mates saw Torquay United rooted to the bottom of the league for the whole season. Only Stevenage Borough's failure to gain approval for their ground ensured league survival for the Gulls. With the top teams in the Vauxhall Conference now ensuring that their grounds meet league standards, it is unlikely that the team finishing bottom in 1996/97 will be similarly reprieved.

# TOTTENHAM HOTSPUR

## White Hart Lane, 748 High Road, Tottenham, London N17 0AP

**Tel No:** 0181 365 5000
**Advance Tickets Tel No:** 0181 365 5050
**League:** F. A. Premier
**Brief History:** Founded 1882 as 'Hotspur', changed name to Tottenham Hotspur in 1885. Former Grounds: Tottenham Marshes and Northumberland Park, moved to White Hart Lane in 1899. F. A. Cup winner 1901 (as a non-League club). Record attendance 75,038
**(Total) Current Capacity:** 32,960 (all seated)
**Visiting Supporters' Allocation:** 4,000
**Club Colours:** White shirts, navy blue shorts
**Nearest Railway Station:** White Hart Lane plus Seven Sisters & Manor House (tube)

**Parking (Car):** Street parking (min ¼ mile from ground)
**Parking (Coach/Bus):** Northumberland Park coach park
**Police Force and Tel No:** Metropolitan (0181 801 3443)
**Disabled Visitors' Facilities**
   **Wheelchairs:** North and South Stands (by prior arrangement)
   **Blind:** No special facility
**Anticipated Development(s):** The club is intending to redevelop the North Stand at the end of the 1996/97 season.

*KEY*
**C** Club Offices
**S** Club Shop
**E** Entrance(s) for visiting supporters
**R** Refreshment bars for visiting supporters
**T** Toilets for visiting supporters

↑ North direction (approx)

❶ Park Lane
❷ A1010 High Road
❸ White Hart Lane BR Station
❹ Paxton Road
❺ Worcester Avenue
❻ West Stand
❼ South Stand

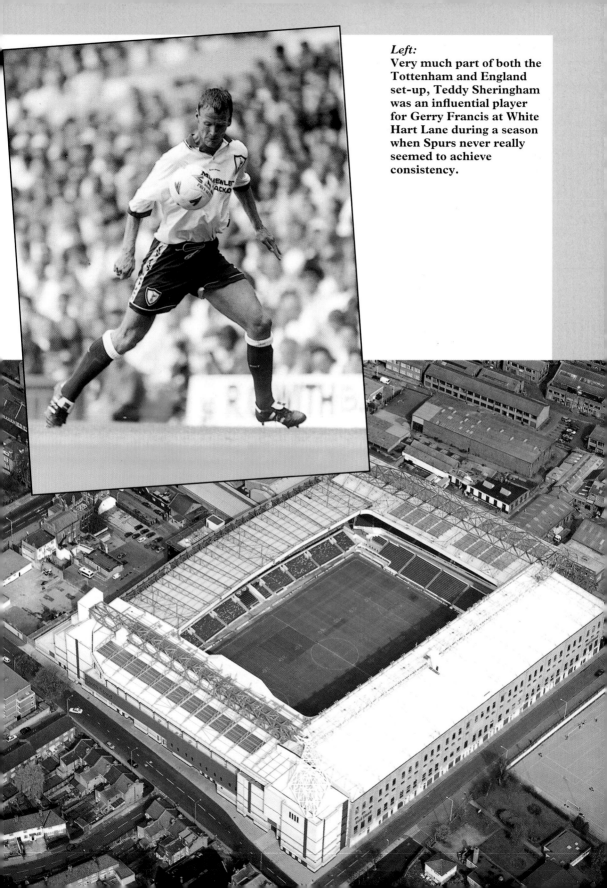

*Left:*
**Very much part of both the Tottenham and England set-up, Teddy Sheringham was an influential player for Gerry Francis at White Hart Lane during a season when Spurs never really seemed to achieve consistency.**

# TRANMERE ROVERS

## Prenton Park, Prenton Road West, Birkenhead, L42 9PN

**Tel No:** 0151 608 4194
**Advance Tickets Tel No:** 0151 609 0137
**League:** 1st Division
**Brief History:** Founded 1884 as Belmont F.C., changed name to Tranmere Rovers in 1885 (not connected to earlier 'Tranmere Rovers'). Former grounds: Steele's Field and Ravenshaw's Field (also known as Old Prenton Park, ground of Tranmere Rugby Club), moved to (new) Prenton Park in 1911. Founder-members 3rd Division North (1921). Record attendance 24,424.

**(Total) Current capacity:** 16,912 (all seated)

**Visiting Supporters' Allocation:** Between 2,000 and 5,823 (all seated)
**Club Colours:** White shirts, white shorts
**Nearest Railway Station:** Hamilton Square or Rock Ferry
**Parking (Car):** Car park at Ground
**Parking (Coach/Bus):** Car park at Ground
**Police Force and Tel No:** Merseyside (0151 709 6010)
**Disabled Visitors' Facilities**
   **Wheelchairs:** Main Stand
   **Blind:** No special facility

### KEY

**C** Club Offices
**S** Club Shop
**E** Entrance(s) for visiting supporters
**R** Refreshment bars for visiting supporters
**T** Toilets for visiting supporters

⬆ North direction (approx)

❶ Car Park
❷ Prenton Road West
❸ Borough Road
❹ M53 Junction 4 (B5151) – 3 miles
❺ Birkenhead (1 mile)

170

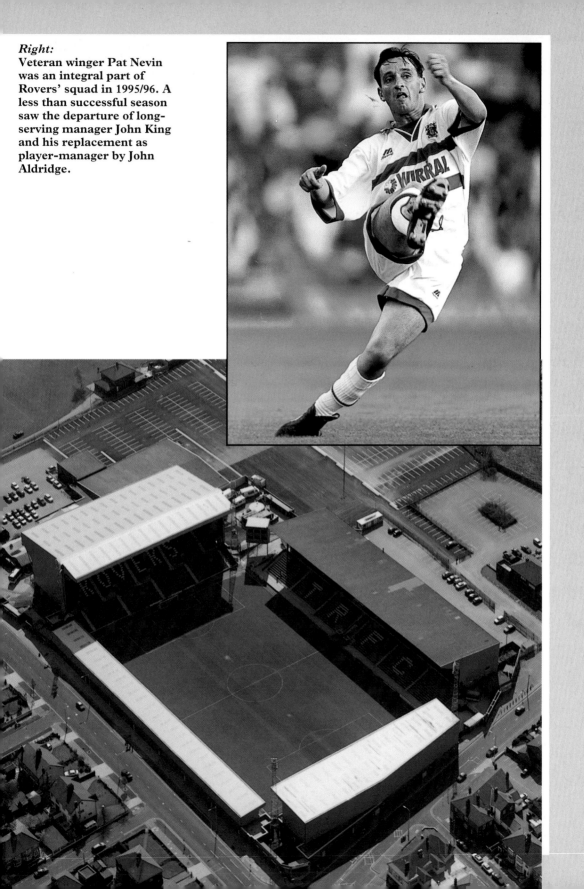

*Right:*
**Veteran winger Pat Nevin was an integral part of Rovers' squad in 1995/96. A less than successful season saw the departure of long-serving manager John King and his replacement as player-manager by John Aldridge.**

# WALSALL

## Bescot Stadium, Bescot Crescent, Walsall, West Midlands, WS1 4SA

**Tel No:** 01922 22791
**Advance Tickets Tel No:** 01922 22791
**League:** 2nd Division
**Brief History:** Founded 1888 as Walsall Town Swifts (amalgamation of Walsall Town - founded 1884 - and Walsall Swifts - founded 1885), changed name to Walsall in 1895. Former Grounds: The Chuckery, West Bromwich Road (twice), Hilary Street (later named Fellows Park, twice), moved to Bescot Stadium in 1990. Founder-members Second Division (1892). Record attendance 10,628 (24,100 at Fellows Park).

**(Total) Current Capacity:** 9,000 (6,700 seated)
**Visiting Supporters' Allocation:** 1,916 (1,916 seated)
**Club Colours:** Red shirts, Black shorts
**Nearest Railway Station:** Bescot
**Parking (Car):** Car park at Ground
**Parking (Coach/Bus):** Car park at Ground
**Police Force and Tel No :** West Midlands (01922 38111)
**Disabled Visitors' Facilities**
  **Wheelchairs:** Highgate Stand
  **Blind:** No special facility

*KEY*

**C** Club Offices
**S** Club Shop
**E** Entrance(s) for visiting supporters
**R** Refreshment bars for visiting supporters
**T** Toilets for visiting supporters

↑ North direction (approx)

❶ Motorway M6
❷ M6 Junction 9
❸ Bescot BR Station
❹ Car Parks
❺ Bescot Crescent

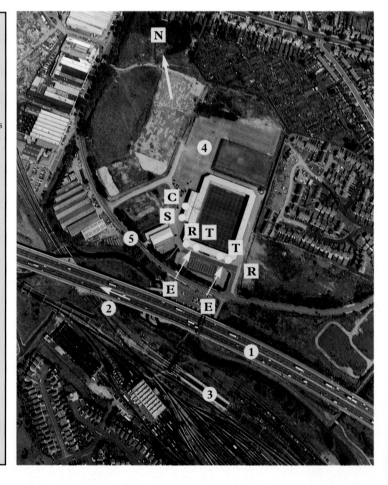

*Left:*
**Following their promotion
the previous year, Walsall
had a season of
consolidation in the 2nd
Division. Saddlers' Kyle
Lightbourne appears to be
contemplating an
imaginary career in the
music business.
Presumably, Walsall's
reserves have shirts
emblazoned 'Second
Choice Personnel'.**

# WATFORD

## Vicarage Road Stadium, Watford, WD1 8ER

**Tel No:** 01923 496000
**Advance Tickets Tel No:** 01923 496010
**League:** 2nd Division
**Brief History:** Founded 1898 as an amalgamation of West Herts (founded 1891) and Watford St. Mary's (founded early 1890s). Former Grounds: Wiggenhall Road (Watford St. Mary's) and West Herts Sports Ground, moved to Vicarage Road in 1922. Founder-members Third Division (1920). Record attendance 34,099.
**(Total) Current Capacity:** 22,000 (all seated)
**Visiting Supporters' Allocation:** 3,500
**Club Colours:** Yellow shirts with black collar & shoulder panel, Black shorts with yellow & red trim.

**Nearest Railway Station:** Watford High Street or Watford Junction.

**Parking (Car):** Nearby multi-storey car park in town centre (10 mins walk)

**Parking (Coach/Bus):** Cardiff Road car park

**Police Force and Tel No:** Hertfordshire (01923 244444)

**Disabled Visitors' Facilities**

**Wheelchairs:** Corner East Stand and South Stand (special enclosure for approx. 24 wheelchairs), plus enclosure in North East Corner

**Blind:** Commentary available in the East Stand (20 seats, free of charge)

---

**KEY**

**C** Club Offices
**S** Club Shop
**E** Entrance(s) for visiting supporters
**R** Refreshment bars for visiting supporters
**T** Toilets for visiting supporters

↑ North direction (approx)

**❶** Vicarage Road
**❷** Occupation Road
**❸** Rous Stand
**❹** Town Centre (¹/₂ mile) – Car Parks, High Street BR Station

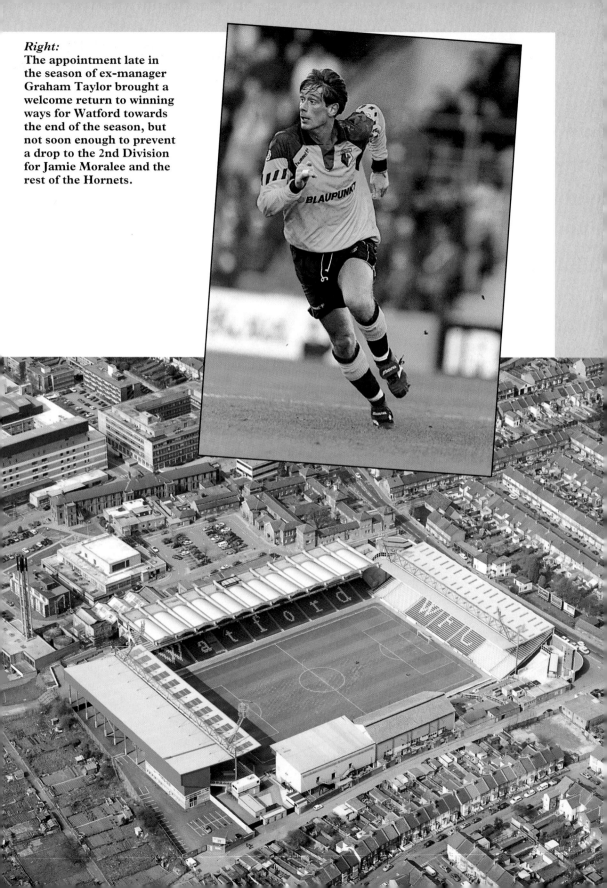

*Right:*
**The appointment late in the season of ex-manager Graham Taylor brought a welcome return to winning ways for Watford towards the end of the season, but not soon enough to prevent a drop to the 2nd Division for Jamie Moralee and the rest of the Hornets.**

# WEST BROMWICH ALBION

## The Hawthorns, Halfords Lane, West Bromwich, West Midlands, B71 4LF

**Tel No:** 0121 525 8888
**Advance Tickets Tel No:** 0121 553 5472
**League:** 1st Division
**Brief History:** Founded 1879. Former Grounds: Coopers Hill, Dartmouth Park, Four Acres, Stoney Lane, moved to the Hawthorns in 1900. Founder-members of Football League (1888). Record attendance 64,815.
**(Total) Current Capacity:** 25,000 (all seated)
**Visiting Supporters' Allocation:** 2,100
**Club Colours:** Navy blue & white striped shirts, white shorts

**Nearest Railway Station:** Rolfe Street, Smethwick (1½ miles)
**Parking (Car):** Halfords Lane & Rainbow Stand car parks.
**Parking (Coach/Bus):** Rainbow Stand car park
**Police Force and Tel No:** West Midlands (0121 554 3414)
**Disabled Visitors' Facilities**
  **Wheelchairs:** Apollo 2000 and West Midlands Travel Community Stands
  **Blind:** Facility available

### KEY
**C** Club Offices
**S** Club Shop
**E** Entrance(s) for visiting supporters
**T** Toilets for visiting supporters

↑ North direction (approx)

❶ A41 Birmingham Road
❷ M5 Junction 1
❸ Birmingham centre (4 miles)
❹ Halfords Lane
❺ Main Stand
❻ Smethwick End
❼ Rolfe Street, Smethwick BR Station (1½ miles)
❽ The Hawthorns BR Station

*Left:*
**Favoured club of one
presenter of *Fantasy
Football League*, the
Baggies had a steady, if
unspectacular, 1st Division
season in 1995/96. West
Brom's Bob Taylor looks
as though he is trying for a
fast track return to the
Premiership.**

# WEST HAM UNITED

## Boleyn Ground, Green Street, Upton Park, London, E13 9AZ

**Tel No:** 0181 548 2748
**Advance Tickets Tel No:** 0181 548 2700
**League:** F. A. Premier
**Brief History:** Founded 1895 as Thames
Ironworks, changed name to West Ham United
in 1900. Former Grounds: Hermit Road,
Browning Road, The Memorial Ground,
moved to Boleyn Ground in 1904. Record
attendance 42,322.
**(Total) Current Capacity:** 25,985 (all seated)
**Visiting Supporters' Allocation:** 3,700
**Club Colours:** Claret & blue shirts, white shorts.
**Nearest Railway Station:** Barking BR, Upton
Park (tube)

**Parking (Car):** Street parking

**Parking (Coach/Bus):** As directed by police

**Police Force and Tel No:** Metropolitan (0181
593 8232)

**Disabled Visitors' Facilities**
　**Wheelchairs:** Green Street
　**Blind:** No special facility

### KEY

**C** Club Offices
**S** Club Shop
**E** Entrance(s) for visiting
　supporters
**R** Refreshment bars for visiting
　supporters
**T** Toilets for visiting supporters

↑ North direction (approx)

❶ A124 Barking Road
❷ Green Street
❸ North Bank
❹ Upton Park Tube Station
　(1/4 mile)
❺ Barking BR Station (1 mile)

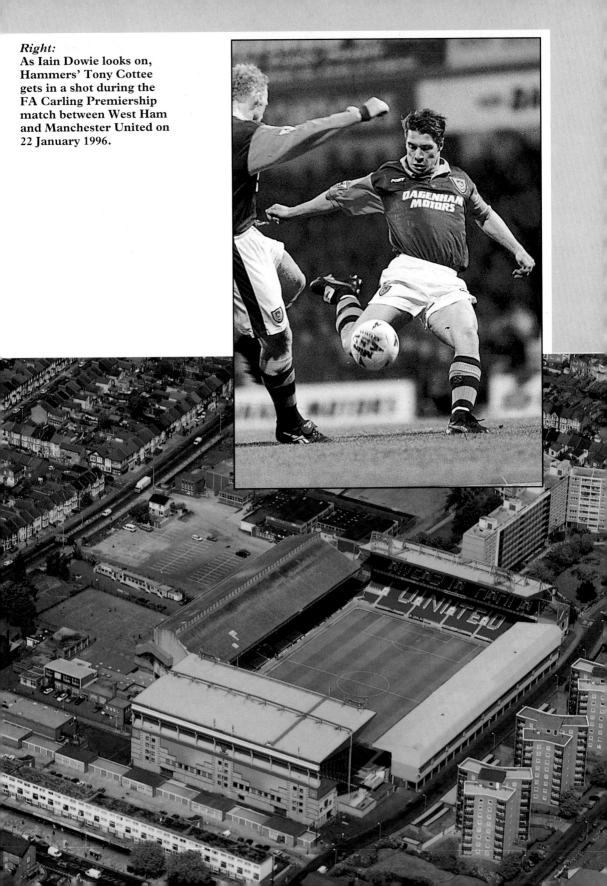

*Right:*
**As Iain Dowie looks on, Hammers' Tony Cottee gets in a shot during the FA Carling Premiership match between West Ham and Manchester United on 22 January 1996.**

# WIGAN ATHLETIC

## Springfield Park, Wigan, Lancs, WN6 7BA

**Tel No:** 01942 244433
**Advance Tickets Tel No:** 01942 244433
**League:** 3rd Division
**Brief History:** Founded 1932. Springfield Park used by former club Wigan Borough (Football League 1921-31) but unrelated to current club. Elected to Football League in 1978 (the last club to be elected rather than promoted). Record attendance 27,500.
**(Total) Current Capacity:** 6,674 (1,109 seated)
**Visiting Supporters' Allocation:** 1,600 (300 seated)
**Club Colours:** Blue and white stripes shirt, blue shorts
**Nearest Railway Station:** Wallgate and North Western (1 mile)

**Parking (Car):** Street parking
**Parking (Coach/Bus):** At Ground
**Police Force and Tel No:** Greater Manchester (01942 244981)
**Disabled Visitors' Facilities**
  **Wheelchairs:** Phoenix Stand side
  **Blind:** Commentary available, book in advance and bring own headphones.
**Anticipated Development(s):** The club is planning, along with the town's Rugby League club, to move into a new 25,000 all-seater stadium. Timescale is uncertain, but the club will continue to play at Springfield Park for at least another two seasons.

*KEY*
**C** Club Offices
**E** Entrance(s) for visiting supporters
**R** Refreshment bars for visiting supporters
**T** Toilets for visiting supporters

↑ North direction (approx)

❶ Private Car Park
❷ Springfield Road
❸ St. Andrews Drive
❹ Wallgate and North Western BR Stations (1 mile)

*Left:*
**One of the most surprising aspects of the 3rd Division in 1995/96 was the presence of a number of Spanish players, like Istro Diaz, in the Wigan team. One wonders what those players used to the climate of the Iberian peninsula made of the Lancashire winter?**

# WIMBLEDON

## Selhurst Park, London, SE25 6PY

**Tel No:** 0181 771 2233
**Advance Tickets Tel No:** 0181 771 8841
**League:** F.A. Premier
**Brief History:** Founded 1889 as Wimbledon Old Centrals, changed name to Wimbledon in 1905. Former Grounds: Wimbledon Common, Pepy's Road, Grand Drive, Merton Hall Road, Malden Wanderers Cricket Ground & Plough Lane. Moved to Selhurst Park (Crystal Palace F.C. Ground) in 1991. Elected to Football League in 1977. Record attendance (Plough Lane) 18,000.
**(Total) Current Capacity:** 26,309 (all seated)
**Visiting Supporters' Allocation:** Approx 3,000
**Club Colours:** Blue shirts, blue shorts

**Nearest Railway Station:** Selhurst, Norwood Junction & Thornton Heath
**Parking (Car):** Street parking & Sainsbury's car park
**Parking (Coach/Bus):** Thornton Heath
**Police Force and Tel No:** Metropolitan (0181 649 1391)
**Disabled Visitors' Facilities**
  **Wheelchairs:** Park Road
  **Blind:** Commentary available
**Anticipated Development(s):** Nothing confirmed following the completion of the Holmesdale Stand. As to whether Wimbledon will continue to play at Selhurst Park, nothing has yet been decided.

### KEY

- **C** Club Offices
- **S** Club Shop
- **E** Entrance(s) for visiting supporters
- **T** Toilets for visiting supporters

↑ North direction (approx)

❶ Whitehorse Lane
❷ Park Road
❸ A213 Selhurst Road
❹ Selhurst BR Station (1/2 mile)
❺ Norwood Junction BR Station (1/4 mile)
❻ Thornton Heath BR Station (1/2 mile)
❼ Car Park (Sainsbury's)
❽ Holmesdale Stand

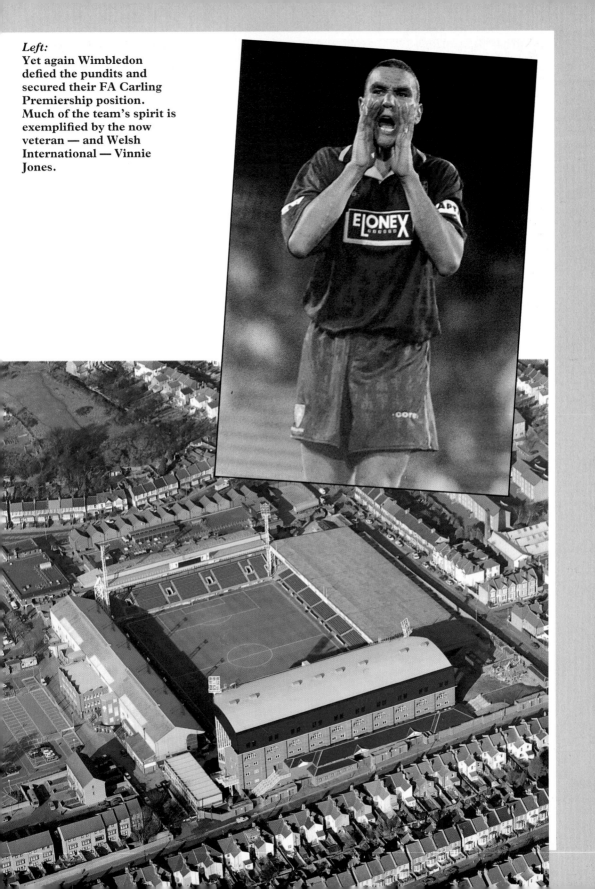

*Left:*
**Yet again Wimbledon defied the pundits and secured their FA Carling Premiership position. Much of the team's spirit is exemplified by the now veteran — and Welsh International — Vinnie Jones.**

# WOLVERHAMPTON WANDERERS

## Molineux Ground, Waterloo Road, Wolverhampton, WV1 4QR

**Tel No:** 01902 655000
**Advance Tickets Tel No:** 01902 653653
**League:** 1st Division
**Brief History:** Founded 1877 as St. Lukes, combined with Goldthorn Hill to become Wolverhampton Wanderers in 1884. Former Grounds: Old Windmill Field, John Harper's Field and Dudley Road, moved to Molineux in 1889. Founder-members Football League (1888). Record attendance 61,315
**(Total) Current Capacity:** 28,500 (all seated)
**Visiting Supporters' Allocation:** 1,500 minimum

**Club Colours:** Gold shirts, black shorts
**Nearest Railway Station:** Wolverhampton
**Parking (Car):** West Park and adjacent North Bank
**Parking (Coach/Bus):** As directed by Police
**Police Force and Tel No:** West Midlands (01902 27851)
**Disabled Visitors' Facilities**
  **Wheelchairs:** 115 places on three sides
  **Blind:** Commentary (by prior arrangement)

### KEY
**C** Club Offices
**S** Club Shop
**E** Entrance(s) for visiting supporters
**R** Refreshment bars for visiting supporters
**T** Toilets for visiting supporters

↑ North direction (approx)

❶ Stan Cullis Stand
❷ John Ireland Stand
❸ Billy Wright Stand
❹ Ring Road – St. Peters
❺ Waterloo Road
❻ A449 Stafford Street
❼ BR Station (¹/2 mile)

*Left:*
A season that promised much for high-spending Wolves saw the much-fancied team fail to live up to expectations, bringing with it the resignation of ex-manager Graham Taylor. One constant in the Wolves set-up for many years has been Steve Bull; this immensely popular striker will lead the Wolves' forward line into the new season and will, no doubt, hope that his endeavours will bring a well-deserved promotion to the top flight.

# WREXHAM

## Racecourse Ground, Mold Road, Wrexham, Clwyd LL11 2AN

**Tel No:** 01978 262129
**Advance Tickets Tel No:** 01978 262129
**League:** 2nd Division
**Brief History:** Founded 1873 (oldest Football Club in Wales). Former Ground: Acton Park, permanent move to Racecourse Ground c.1900. Founder-members Third Division North (1921). Record attendance 34,445.
**(Total) Current Capacity:** 12,500 (5,026 seated)
**Visiting Supporters' Allocation:** 2,680 (2,230 seated)

**Club Colours:** Red shirts, white shorts
**Nearest Railway Station:** Wrexham General
**Parking (Car):** (Nearby) Town car parks
**Parking (Coach/Bus):** As directed by Police
**Police Force and Tel No:** Wrexham Division (01978 290222)
**Disabled Visitors' Facilities**
  **Wheelchairs:** Mold Road Side
  **Blind:** No special facility
**Anticipated development(s):** Work is about to start on a new 4,000 seat stand.

### KEY

**C** Club Offices
**S** Club Shop
**E** Entrance(s) for visiting supporters
**R** Refreshment bars for visiting supporters
**T** Toilets for visiting supporters

⬆ North direction (approx)

❶ Wrexham General BR Station
❷ A541 – Mold Road
❸ Wrexham Town Centre
❹ Car Park
❺ Kop Town End

186

**Right: Gary Bennett seen in familiar pose for Wrexham.**

# WYCOMBE WANDERERS

## Adams Park, Hillbottom Road, Sands, High Wycombe, Bucks, HP12 4HJ.

**Tel No:** 01494 472100
**Advance Tickets Tel No:** 01494 441118
**League:** 2nd Division
**Brief History:** Founded 1884. Former Grounds:
The Rye, Spring Meadows, Loakes Park,
moved to Adams Park 1990. Promoted to
Football League 1993. Record attendance
15,678 (Loakes Park)
**(Total) Current Capacity:** 9,600 (1,267 seated)
**Visiting Supporters' Allocation:** 2,200
(standing)
**Club Colours:** Blue with half length stripes and
red trim, Blue shorts.

**Nearest Railway Station:** High Wycombe
($2^{1}/2$ miles)
**Parking (Car):** At Ground and Street parking
**Parking (Coach/Bus):** At Ground
**Police Force and Tel No:** Thames Valley 01296
396534
**Disabled Visitors' Facilities**
   **Wheelchairs:** Special shelter - Main Stand,
   Hillbottom Road end
   **Blind:** Commentary available
**Anticipated Development(s):** New all-seater
   stand with executive boxes on South side under
   construction.

**KEY**

**C** Club Offices
**S** Club Shop
**E** Entrance(s) for visiting
supporters
**R** Refreshment bars for visiting
supporters
**T** Toilets for visiting supporters

**↑** North direction (approx)

**❶** Car Park
**❷** Hillbottom Road (Industrial
Estate)
**❸** M40 Junction 4 (approx. 2
miles)
**❹** Wycombe Town Centre
(approx. $2^{1}/2$ miles)
**❺** Woodlands Stand

*Left:*
Following the departure of the charismatic manager Martin O'Neill to Norwich, Wycombe Wanderers always seemed likely to find their second season in the 2nd Division a struggle. A number of good performances, however, ensured that the team was never threatened with the drop. John Williams seems in determined mood in this contest.

# YORK CITY

## Bootham Crescent, York, YO3 7AQ

**Tel No:** 01904 624447
**Advance Tickets Tel No:** 01904 624447
**League:** 2nd Division
**Brief History:** Founded 1922. Former ground: Fulfordgate Ground, moved to Bootham Crescent in 1932. Record attendance 28,123.
**(Total) Current Capacity:** 9,459 (3,670 seated)
**Visiting Supporters' Allocation:** 3,500 (630 seated)
**Club Colours:** Red shirts, blue shorts

**Nearest Railway Station:** York
**Parking (Car):** Street parking
**Parking (Coach/Bus):** As directed by Police
**Police Force and Tel No:** North Yorkshire (01904 631321)
**Disabled Visitors' Facilities**
  **Wheelchairs:** In front of Family Stand
  **Blind:** No special facility

### KEY

- **C** Club Offices
- **S** Club Shop
- **E** Entrance(s) for visiting supporters
- **R** Refreshment bars for visiting supporters
- **T** Toilets for visiting supporters

↑ North direction (approx)

❶ Bootham Crescent
❷ Grosvenor Road
❸ Burton Stone Lane
❹ York BR Station (1 mile)

*Right:*
**Just when you thought romance was dead in football, 2nd Division York City proved you wrong by winning in the Coco Cola Cup at mighty Manchester United. Scott Jordan celebrates the triumph. Unfortunately, for York, the rest of the season was less successful, with the club facing a replay behind closed doors against Brighton & Hove Albion — the first match was abandoned due to crowd violence at the Goldstone Ground — to ensure 2nd Division survival.**

 Aerofilms

Aerofilms was founded in 1919 and has specialised in the acquisition of aerial photography within the United Kingdom throughout its history. The company has a record of being innovative in the uses and applications of aerial photography.

Photographs looking at the environment in perspective are called oblique aerial photographs. These are taken with Hasselblad cameras by professional photographers experienced in the difficult conditions encountered in aerial work.

Photographs looking straight down at the landscape are termed vertical aerial photographs. These photographs are obtained using Leica survey cameras, the products from which are normally used in the making of maps.

Aerofilms has a unique library of oblique and vertical photographs in excess of one and a half million in number covering the United Kingdom. This library of photographs dates from 1919 to the present and is continually being updated.

Oblique and vertical photography can be taken to customers' specification by Aerofilms' professional photographers.

To discover more of the wealth of past or present photographs held in the library at Aerofilms or to commission new aerial photography to your requirements, please contact:

Hunting Aerofilms Limited
Gate Studios
Station Road
Borehamwood
Herts WD6 1EJ

Telephone 0181-207-0666
Fax 0181-207-5433